Haunted Indianapolis

And Other Indiana Ghost Stories

Tom Baker and Jonathan Titchenal

Schiffer Publishing Ltd®

4880 Lower Valley Road, Atglen, Pennsylvania 19310

Published by Schiffer Publishing Ltd.
4880 Lower Valley Road
Atglen, PA 19310
Phone: (610) 593-1777; Fax: (610) 593-2002
E-mail: Info@schifferbooks.com

For the largest selection of fine reference books on this and related
subjects, please visit our web site at www.schifferbooks.com. We are
always looking for people to write books on new and related subjects.
If you have an idea for a book please contact us at the above address.

This book may be purchased from the publisher.
Include $3.95 for shipping.
Please try your bookstore first.
You may write for a free catalog.

In Europe, Schiffer books are distributed by
Bushwood Books
6 Marksbury Ave.
Kew Gardens
Surrey TW9 4JF England
Phone: 44 (0) 20 8392-8585; Fax: 44 (0) 20 8392-9876
E-mail: info@bushwoodbooks.co.uk
Website: www.bushwoodbooks.co.uk
Free postage in the U.K., Europe; air mail at cost.

Designed by "Sue"
Type set in A Charming Font/NewBskvll BT

ISBN: 978-0-7643-2747-6
Printed in China

Contents

Part Two—Stories by Jonathan Titchenal

Introduction
by Tom Baker

The subject of ghosts is one that is near and dear to me: As a person that has experienced supernatural phenomena, I know that ghosts do, indeed, exist in some fashion. Whether they represent the souls of departed human beings, the "flicker effect" from a distortion in the space-time continuum, or simply a change in the psychological perception of those sensitive persons who wander into a reputedly "haunted" area, is irrelevant. The phenomena itself is beyond dispute.

That coming to a decisive conclusion regarding the objective reality of any story in this hysterical day and age seems fraught with the severest of obstacles, goes without saying. To more fully define what life is, and in a sense, what it means to be a fully cognizant individual and a participating conscious ego at this moment of time requires us to look into many dark and troubling spaces. To peer beyond the mundane, workaday reality that imprisons us, we must be willing to forego any preconceived notions we may have of what is true and untrue, possible and impossible, reality and dream.

This particular journey finds us traveling the dust-choked back roads and lonely little burgs of the great State of Indiana, in search of rare and wonderful legends and lore; anecdotes and mysteries. The entire journey has been planned and pursued through the course of this little volume to help us come to a better understanding of what we are, and where we came from (and where some of us are going).

Indiana has been occupied since nearly the beginning of the Christian era: various and sundry bands of Natives used the land and saw it as their own sacred place well before white settlers ever broke ground. Taken from the hands of natives, the land was conquered by the French, given over to the British, and finally handed over to the American Revolutionary government where it was declared a state in 1816.

As a fertile "breadbasket," Indiana Territory was ripe for the pioneering spirit of farmers looking to move into the Northwest and gain their living by toiling in the good black earth that had once been the sacred soil of Shawnee and Miami Indians. The "log cabin" history of the state is as sure as its vast waves of gently blowing fields, dilapidated barns, and deep, wooded places.

It is a history of a people made of stern stuff, of folks moving in covered wagons over a land they hoped to tame and make profitable. It is a history of dusty, lonely little towns, of iron hard hands splitting the raw earth in hopes of making it give forth precious crops, of old farm houses, weed-choked cemeteries, and the past flowing as easily into the future as the rays of sunset fade into the twinkling eerie cold of nightfall.

This is Indiana: A land of little churches, tiny houses, vacant factories, working class values, and small cities that seem perched forevermore on the dimensional cusp separating the era of horse-drawn carriages from the modern world of computers, cell phones, and color *TV*.

Indiana, while never a "slave state," still suffered from a history of intense racism and bigotry. During the early twenties, Indiana was the national seat of the Ku Klux Klan, with prestigious members of local and state government all wearing the flowing white bed sheets and carrying the blood-red shield of racial hatred, and fighting, against the flow of history, to keep the races "separate but equal." A telling example of this is taken from Alistair Cooke's *America*, in which a horrific photograph of a lynching is paired with a caption suggesting that the event actually happened somewhere in the "deep South." In actuality, the lynching took place on the steps of the Marion, Indiana courthouse.

It is this past, this secret, buried history of hardship and intolerance, which gives rise to so many legends of ghosts. Every moment of tragedy or hope that befalls man, whether it be the accidental death of a child, the murder by an angry mob of a man wrongfully accused, or simply the sacred sense of presence that exists in the old boards of a historic home or the gentle dip of hills, brings to life a sense of connection with the past. With the Dead.

The authors of this work aim to recount, for your edification as well as mystification, a short litany of spectral phantasms and baffling "bumps in the night." We hope to take you with us as we travel the dimly lit hallways of old hotels, walk black pathways between overarching trees as the moonlight creates spectral faces on the shoulder of the asphalt, and let you live the nightmare of one anonymous family, whose long-dead Great Uncle refused to let go of his former lodgings.

Together, we will walk the grounds of historic Camp Chesterfield, the "Hub of American Spiritualism," and travel backward through the decades to recount the hair-raising tale of an Indiana minister and his standoff with the powers of darkness.

We'll plod around the quiet earth in search of Belle Gunness, famed "black widow" and killer of hopeful husbands, who disappeared without a trace, and who, some say, has decided to return once more to the beloved plot of land where once she reigned in bloody fervor.

We will tell you a comic tale of a neurotic business-man, in hopes that the next time you hear the phone ring, a chill will settle down your spine. We will walk with you across a fateful bridge to see what waits in the cemetery beyond.

All of this awaits you, dear reader, as you turn the pages of this little tome and enter into the land where the dead walk, speak, and even love.

So put out the overhead lights, lock the doors, bolt the shutters, and settle into that comfortable chair you keep in the corner. Make sure you are alone.

Outside, the wind has picked up, a little. The moon is shining fat and furiously over the rolling fields, beaming off the trickling brooks, and letting loose its secrets for us tonight.

Are you ready?

Then let us begin...

Wait... What's that noise?!

Author's Note

This text has been divided into two sections. The first, written by Tom Baker, is made up primarily of stories and folklore. The second, written by Jonathan Titchenal, focuses more on investigations and docu-mented accounts.

Part One

Stories by

Tom Baker

Uncle Orrin

The family had lived in the old house at the top of the hill for time out of mind. It had sheltered generations within its crumbling interior, and stood at the top of the street like a grim sentinel, surrounded by houses equally weathered.

Above them, the surrounding hills divided as they sloped to meet the street, a train trestle standing guard above. It was a short walk through the backyard and up the steep hillside to get to the top of the tracks. Mind you, not that anyone wanted to be standing there when a train came rumbling by.

The house had been owned by a family named Everett, and the matron of the family had the luck late in life to be blessed with a son. Orrin Everett was a tall, blond haired, brown-eyed boy with a sleepy look in his eyes and a helpful nature.

As a tot, he had been sickly, and had been fussed over constantly by his worried mother and her gaggle of sisters, all of whom had fallen instantly in love with the boy.

They had nursed him to a robust health, and as young child, he found his greatest delight in roaming around the backyard on tottering little legs, basking in the warm sunlight and gentle breezes of childhood's most special moments. Then, as sure of himself as he could possibly be, he clambered up the rickety stone steps of the back porch, liking the way the boards creaked beneath his little shoes.

This was all in the gentle years before the First World War. The boy seemed to shoot upward at an alarming rate. Tall and good-looking, Orrin excelled in sports, hated studying, and liked nothing better than to lie back in the grass, or sit on the porch on a hot summer day, drinking his lemonade from an old mason jar. The clouds rolled by, and, in his mind, Orrin built mansions in the heavens and kingdoms made of sky.

The family, across the span of the years, had lost their patriarch, so that now the only male living in the house—besides an incredibly aged grandfather named Bill—was Orrin. Orrin had taken it hard when his father had been killed in an accident at his job in a local glass factory, and had wept inconsolably for days at a time.

When nightfall came on, and he finally tiptoed down the creaking staircase to claim his cold dinner, Grandfather Bill fancied he could see a strange change come over the boy's gaunt, unhappy features. It was only after sundown that he ceased to mourn, and instead puttered around quietly, lost in some world where pain and death could not reach him.

His mother, to be blunt, was worried sick.

He had completely quit school, and now spent most of his days lost in a melancholy reverie, seeming as if he was just on the verge of working something out with himself, and then immediately retreating again into the perpetual gloom of his sullen quiet. It was a difficult, jarring time in Orrin's life, and it was about to get worse.

His mother was gentle with him in her own manner, but eventually, realizing that only he would be able to work himself free of the perpetual sorrow that had descended upon him like a black shroud, decided to leave him alone with his own troubles. She threw herself into her new job, knowing it was going to take every extra penny they could muster just to keep the family afloat.

In time, Orrin did begin to slowly find his own sense of inner-strength, and slowly forgot the death of his father. Unfortunately for the boy, he was soon to learn that his new stepfather was none too fond of him.

Whatever possessed Orrin's mother to marry the man is anyone's guess, but he proved to be a stern, domineering tyro straight out of a lurid novel. Although he had appeared to be every bit the kind, considerate man during the short romance and courtship, after marriage his true personality began to shine out with disturbing clarity.

He was often drunk, and even when he was sober, he proved an impatient, abusive bully. He treated his new wife badly, and he bitterly hated her young son with a passion. Once, when both he and his wife were gone for the day, Orrin thought he would do a good deed to win the affection of his new parent. He carefully scrubbed the kitchen floor, unthinkingly using corrosive lye to do so. When the couple returned and found that the kitchen floor was ruined, the man was furious. He viciously beat the boy, then made him strip naked and scrub the floor again to perfection, beating him with a leather strap as he did so. Orrin's mother was horrified, and it was not long after that she divorced her abusive husband, throwing him out and trying, as best she could, to make peace with her son.

As the years wore on, and duty called, Orrin was eventually drafted to fight in the Great War in France, to the horror of his mother, who was sure he would never make it home alive. Admirably, he swallowed his fear and went, leaving home for the first time in his life, and surviving many close brushes with death.

Every night of his absence, Orrin's mother knelt at the side of her old bed, and prayed that the hands of the Lord would be upon him as he tarried in the Ardennes Forest. Once, in one of his many letters home, Orrin related how he had been sitting in the trenches, eating with his men, when suddenly a small voice seemed to insist to him that he get up and move to the opposite side. He got up and walked away, just as a mortar came screaming down out of the air, killing everyone in that end of the trench. He had turned white, realizing that he had been spared being blown to bits.

It was anecdotes like these that kept his mother faithfully anticipating his return from the Front.

Of course, he did suffer an injury to his legs which sent him home permanently, but in time he learned to overcome his difficulties and even get up and about. He began to seemingly put the war behind him. In time, and with a firm regimen of exercise and a positive mental attitude, he surprised his family by returning to work, telling them: "It isn't meant for a man just to lay about and do nothing. If that is all the future holds, I might as well be dead." Orrin took a job ringing up a cash register at the corner grocery, before finally, a few years later, joining a construction firm. It seemed that his healing was finally complete.

By this time, his mother had remarried for the last time, to a kindly gentleman that liked her rather shy, backward son just fine, and got along with him splendidly. For years, life steadied itself into a new pattern, and seemed as placid as it had been before, if not somewhat financially strained.

It was not long after this that Orrin's mother, while attending a Ladies Christian Auxiliary meeting had occasion to meet a newcomer to the group, who boasted of "spiritualistic faculties" and was adept at the ancient art of reading tea leaves. Orrin's mother, slightly amused, had a reading performed right there during the meeting, and was quite astonished by what the would-be medium pronounced for her in her future.

"I don't know if you'll appreciate knowing this," she said. "But I see a death in your family."

Astonished, the mother implored the medium to tell her any details concerning the tragedy, and was rewarded with this:

> "I see a man laying in a bed of roses. He's a young man, and he's died from an accident of some sort. I can't see any more."

Aghast, Orrin's mother knew in her heart that this could only mean her son, but she, of course, said nothing to him. Imagine her sense of joy and relief when, shortly after this reading, he came to her and said that he was handing in his resignation from work because the pain from his old war injuries was starting to trouble him again.

"I'm going to have to look for a sit-down job, I suppose." Orrin said, rather gloomily. "I suppose any work at all is better than nothing." Orrin liked to work with his hands, and his mind was always on the outdoors and the open sunshine.

Whether or not a sit-down job would have been entirely satisfying to Orrin was an issue that he would never have the opportunity to resolve. It was during what would have been his last week at work that, while working on the renovation of an old pharmacy, Orrin slipped from the scaffolding, his legs apparently having buckled beneath him. He fell several stories into a stony garden. Surrounding his dying body was a rosebush curled in thorny bloom.

His grief-stricken mother mourned herself nearly to death. It was only a short time later that the woman indeed did die, of complications related to surgery. Thus, the house was empty save for her husband. In a short time, a daughter from a former marriage, now married and having several children herself, came to live with him.

The house continued it's encompassing of life, watching from its foundations as days and weeks turned into years. As the present grew into the future, the living family that dwelled there began to realize slowly that the past, although as intangible as a few of Grandpa's tired memories, was not entirely at rest.

It began with Grandpa's insistence that at night he could hear Orrin coming up the back staircase to his room, and that he could hear his heavy work boots and his unusual shuffling gate outside his door at night. The family worried that this might be the first touches of an oncoming senility.

In time, however, they began to see that there was something going on in the old family home besides the occasional creaking of floorboards as the house settled into its decrepitude.

There were three young daughters, all nearly equal in age, and all seemingly terrified by the back upper bedroom that had once belonged to Uncle Orrin. The bedroom was now being used by the youngest daughter, but it was a fight to get her to stay there. The rest of the house, she would claim, always seemed homey, but when she went into the back bedroom, a heaviness and a feeling of dread seemed to settle in upon her. This feeling would grow even worse with the lights off, in the middle of the night.

She too had heard the strange footsteps, and felt the uncanny sense of dread squeeze the breath from her chest as she lay in bed, shivering in terror. She could feel icy fingers crawl across her skin, and see something moving in the dark shadows of her bedroom.

Objects, such as an electric fan or an odd piece of bric-a-brac, would mysteriously vanish, only to appear later in the most unlikely places. The youngest sister, who slept in Orrin's old room, soon refused to sleep anywhere but the couch, and the older sister agreed to trade beds with her.

Her experience was even worse: Lying in bed at night, watching the shadow of a sleek black cat walk across the tree branch outside her window, she fell asleep to strange, troubling dreams, only to awake moments later with a suffocating sensation.

She could hear the little paws of the cat scratch against the ledge below her window as it stopped there, peering in at her with eyes that seemed to glow a luminous evil. A figure seemed to coalesce in the swirling shadows, blacker than black in the moonlight. The figure of a man.

She fought to scream, as outside she heard the cat begin to screech. Suddenly, an oppressive, icy weight seemed to be pressing down on her chest.

She felt the side of the bed press down, as if an invisible weight had suddenly crawled in beside her. Her skin began to tingle and throb under the chilling cold of an invisible touch.

The rest of the family heard her ear-piercing scream, and her father and mother came rushing upstairs and into her room.

She was hysterical, and despite all their assurances that she must have only been dreaming, refused ever again to go in the old back room. Her father tried to dismiss the fears of his family and reassure them that it was a perfectly ordinary old house, and that there was no such thing as ghosts.

One day, while the rest of his family was watching television, he decided to sit for awhile in Orrin's old room and read his Bible. Perhaps he was simply trying to reassure himself.

He sat down on the bed, suddenly feeling the mysterious cold that seemed to linger in the room, and opened the book. He found, though, that he couldn't concentrate on the words, and as the shadows began to lengthen from the setting sun, he felt the strange sense of suffocation grip his chest and stop his words in his throat. He knelt immediately to pray, but just as he tremblingly bent across the surface of the bed and folded his hands, he heard a strange slithering hiss come stealing from a darkened corner. He stared in rapt terror as a long, coiling shadow-thing began to move across the floor toward him.

He wasted little time in getting to his feet, shaking and backing away as he looked into the darkness. It had only been a mirage, he thought. Certainly it was nothing more than his nerves, and a trick of the light. But after that, he avoided going into the back room unless absolutely necessary.

Whatever presence haunted the back room, it seemed to treat the youngest daughter the worst: she one day told her family that while putting on her socks, she had heard three knocks coming from inside her closet. That the closet had once been a doorway accessible by the back staircase, and had only been modified in recent years, was something her family chose not to tell her.

Of course, she also told them that the Devil had spoken to her once, in the middle of the night, speaking softly from the same corner of the room from where she had seen the black apparition. In time, she would forget many things about the old house, but this secret conversation she would never forget. Neither would she confide the particulars concerning what was discussed.

By the time the family finally found it financially feasible to move, there was a new grandson. The family had grown, and the oldest daughter was on her own. Life went on unabated, without the bizarre happenings that had centered on the former family home.

Eventually, they got word that it had burned down quite mysteriously, a presumed electrical fire suddenly engulfing part of the house and making it worthy of little more than demolition. A vacant lot resides there now.

The fire, incidentally, started in the back bedroom.

Scratches

Marion, Indiana is a quiet, sober town that some would say has seen better days. With the closure of several factories, and an increasing tide of unemployment, the residents of Marion, as of late, have found themselves hanging onto hope with a bitter determination that one day they would be able to see their small city rise again and reclaim its former glory.

However, while presently jobs in Marion may have grown scarce, it has never in its long history had a shortage of churches. Most varieties of Christianity are represented in Marion (which has the distinction of being the birthplace, oddly enough, of "rebel" movie actor James Dean), and the populace is overwhelmingly conservative in religious appetite as well as political philosophy.

The Wesleyan denomination predominates, if for no other reason than the single fact that Indiana Wesleyan University has its campus headquartered nearly on the outskirts of town. Although you will certainly find Catholics, Presbyterians, Methodists, Mormons, Pentecostals, Mennonites, Seventh Day Adventists, a smattering of Spiritualists, and even a few displaced Pagans, as well as a handful of Jewish families, the Wesleyans and Baptists have it.

Thus, Sunday services are well-attended events, marking not only the passing of weeks into months, and months into years, but also allowing folks a reprieve to join in fellowship once a week with like-minded people. It may not be Big City Thrills, but it's mighty homey.

It was during just such a Sunday service, when the Pastor (We'll call him Reverend Trask), finished his sermon with a soft prayer, said the Benediction, and walked from the pulpit to the front door to shake hands with his parishioners as they filed out.

As the last of the parishioners left the comfort and sanctuary of the old church, he noticed a peculiar woman standing in the foyer. She was wearing a respectable blue dress, carrying a handbag, and looking for all the world as if she had just lost her oldest and dearest friend.

Soon the congregation had all departed, and the minister was left alone in the outer vestibule with the woman. She approached him, a little cautiously, and then held out her hand, saying: "Hello. I know you don't know me...but I have no where else to turn."

She instantly broke down sobbing, and the minister drew her close, putting his hand on her arm and telling her, "We can speak in my office, if you like. Just follow me."

They went into his office, closed the door behind him, and sat down heavily behind his desk. Although watching over his flock sometimes was a tiring duty, he never failed to appreciate their wants and concerns. His was a twenty-four hour position, but he did his utmost to fill it to the best of his ability.

The woman wiped her eyes with a handkerchief, and then said, in a trembling voice: "Pastor, it's my husband. Something is wrong with him...I can't explain it. He won't sleep, he won't eat. He barely speaks to me anymore. And last night he woke me up out of a sound sleep, growling something about hearing strange voices and scratches in the room. Well, I listened, and I couldn't hear anything. But this morning, as I lay in bed, I could feel the most oppressive sense of...of evil that I have ever felt in my life. I am not a religious person at all. I've never even been here before, as a matter of fact, and my husband says he doesn't even believe in God. I had to get out of that house today, so I went for a drive, and when I came by here, and saw all the cars outside, something just told me that I should come and talk to you."

The minister sat back in his chair and closed his eyes to mere slits. He was not sure what the problem here was, if it was spiritual or something more mundane that young married people were apt to go through from time to time. It could even be reckoned that the husband or wife were in serious need of psychiatric counseling.

He said, "How would you like me to help you?"

"Could you see him, Reverend? Perhaps come and talk to him? Could you bless our home?"

The Reverend told her, immediately, that he could. As they rode out of town toward the place, the woman filled him in on some of the strange phenomena that had been occurring ever since they had left their former home and moved into the renovated farmhouse. She related a litany of strange, creeping surprises that had foisted themselves upon the family only weeks after they had moved out of their former home.

At first, it had been only small things: at night, while lying in bed next to her husband, the woman swore that she could hear footsteps on the stairs, or rustling around below, in the living room. She would lay awake in a state of abject fear, too scared to even move, her breath gasping in and out. Her husband, a heavy sleeper, usually simply rolled over and murmured to himself.

She might grab his arm, if the noises got to be too loud. Invariably, when he awoke, with a sort of grumbling irritation, he would simply snort with his eyes still closed.

"Mice. I'll get some traps tomorrow, honey. Go back to sleep."

But the noises in the night grew louder, more frequent, until even he couldn't ignore or put them off any longer. Loud, ringing footsteps often awoke them from a dead sleep, and her husband would bound from the bed with his gun, throw open the bedroom door, and rush out to the top of the stairs. Always, they were dark and empty, betraying no hint of an intruder.

It was then that objects began to mysteriously vanish and reappear in odd places: Keys, books, small trinkets would disappear and somehow find themselves in the most unlikely of places. Once, while they were both comfortably ensconced in front of the fireplace, an entire heavy chest of china plates came crashing over onto the kitchen floor. The couple rushed into the room, dodging flying dishes and shards of glass as they whipped crazily around the room, some becoming embedded in the wooden door.

The house would tremble with savage blows, like the thudding fall of heavy stones, and the temperature would veer wildly between boiling hot and freezing cold, sometimes within the same room.

And then there were the scratches.

It was as if several small, feral animals were hiding in the walls, scrabbling across the ceiling with sharp little claws. At first, her husband had tried to dismiss it as simply "mice," and even suggested that squirrels may have built a nest in the roof. He shrugged off any occurrence he couldn't explain; he didn't understand it, he claimed, and what he didn't understand, he didn't want to know about.

He had been eating breakfast one morning, and she had been brewing coffee, when suddenly she turned to see him duck instantly down. He picked his head up again gasping, and looked behind him.

There was a deadly sharp kitchen knife embedded in the wall behind him, its handle still vibrating gently from the force of its projection. He had just narrowly missed having that knife thrust by invisible hand directly into his face.

Just at that moment, as his wife stood there looking aghast at what had just happened, the coffee pot seemingly erupted on the burner, shooting a spray of scalding water. If she had not jumped backward instinctively, she would have been badly burned.

Suddenly, a deafening crash erupted through the living room, as books and trinkets began to fly from the shelves of a large oak case. The case itself had scooted out from the wall, and was suddenly thrust down onto the floor, cracking a portion of its surface. The woman was left in a state of near-shock, and finally refused to be left alone in the house during the day. Her husband seemed baffled about the ominous doings, yet admitted he was still unwilling to move. He, nonetheless, permitted her to accompany him to town each morning, and she whiled away the hours while he was at work visiting shops or reading in the public library.

When the time came for both of them to finally return home in the evening, she felt a knot of fear and loathing curl itself around in the pit of her stomach. The couple would somewhat hesitantly enter, and she would hurry to warm some food for them, keeping her fingers crossed that finally, everything would calm down to a sense of normality. They would then sit sullenly at the dining room table, expecting at any moment some outrageous spectacle, and finally retiring, uneasily, with the comforting hum of the radio tuned to pleasant music in an effort to block out the strange scratching.

As they pulled up in front of the old place, Reverend Trask clutched his Bible tightly in his right hand. The woman continued:

"Every once in a great while, in the night, we would feel something tugging at the covers on the bed. And then there was the night they were pulled completely back, and then pulled off the bed and flung into a corner. I thought that the objects flying through the air were the worst of it, but then a few nights ago, Jack woke me up complaining that something had attacked him while we were sleeping. He showed me scratches on his shirt—"

"Scratches? You mean the thing actually, well, clawed him?"

"Yes," she replied, turning off the car and sitting still for a moment. "And more than once. The same thing happened last night. He said something with glowing eyes came out of the darkness at him. He said it grabbed him while he lay there, too scared to move. I was so exhausted I noticed nothing, but the next thing I know he's out of bed and standing by the window, holding his pistol. Then…"

Her voice fell to stillness.

"He shot it? My God, you could have been killed. He must have been dreaming."

"Oh no. No Sir, he was wide awake and scared out of his mind. We've been married for ten years, and in all that time I've never seen him like this. All he's done for the past two days is lay in bed, looking sick. He says he can feel something fighting for him…fighting for his soul."

She suddenly broke down weeping, and he tried to console her as best he could, but finally stated: "Well, that's not going to help at this point. It's in God's hands now."

As they walked up the drive toward the ramshackle old place, Reverend Trask couldn't help but feel a sense of the boring normality of the exterior. It looked like many older two-story country homes, with a white-washed exterior, a slightly-sagging porch, and an air of homespun gentility. Upon stepping onto the porch, in the comfortable glare of early-afternoon sunshine, he almost decided that the real problem here wasn't any menacing, inexplicable force, but was simply the strain and pressure of marital life driving these young people to conjure up phantasmal evil where none existed. It was, after all, damned hard to be frightened of phantom callers on a bright Sunday afternoon.

If he for an instant thought her claims to be dubious, however, as soon as she opened the door and he stepped foot inside that gloomy old edifice, he realized that, indeed, there was something here that lent itself to creeping unease.

The living room was spacious, and the house itself looked quite nice and tidy. Altogether, as the eye took in the overall surroundings at a glance, it looked like any normal abode of a moderately well-off couple. However, as Reverend Trask followed the woman up the stairs and down the hall into the bedroom, he experienced a cold, clammy feeling steal over him, a sort of mysterious anxiety, and a terrible sadness and suffocation of the spirit. Quite before he set foot into the bedroom, he was choking back a sob of melancholy.

Before him, sitting on the edge of the bed, holding his head in his hands was a very haggard looking younger man still dressed in his pajamas. At the sound of the Reverend entering, the man jerked his head upward, revealing the general appearance of a man who had been losing a lot of sleep—a man that was, perhaps, on the verge of succumbing to a nervous breakdown.

"Pastor, you have to help me. There is a demon that's been attacking me in the night…I tried to shoot it, but you can't kill it. It clawed me across the chest in my sleep!"

With that the man raised his shirt, revealing four jagged cuts, as if an animal had raked its claws across the man's stomach.

Under ordinary circumstances, Reverend Trask might have assumed he was merely dealing with a psychologically disturbed man. However, as he stood in the gloom of the bedroom, looking down at the man, Reverend Trask knew that something of a spiritual, perhaps even supernatural nature, might indeed be occurring.

The man suddenly bounded from the bed, looking more alert than he had when Reverend Trask had first entered. He went to the far wall, pointing at the bullet hole he had shot through it last night.

"It started with the footsteps, and the scratching in the walls. Then objects flying around everywhere, and furniture being moved while we were gone. Then, several nights ago, I saw a black form hovering over my bed. I thought I was still dreaming, but my eyes were wide awake, and I couldn't move. Last night, it tried to kill me…"

Reverend Trask asked the man if he had any faith. Receiving "no" as a reply, he asked the man to sit with him and pray for the release of his home from the grip of whatever low spirit had taken hold there. However, upon kneeling, he soon found himself choking on his words, his mind a sudden cold, biting frost of fear and panic.

"We should be gone from here," said the man, holding his stomach as if, suddenly, it had been gripped by a sharp pain. Reverend Trask got to his feet, clutching his Bible closely, and said: "I think that you may be right. I don't feel like I can stay here in your home much longer. Would you be averse to coming back to the church with me?"

"Why?" asked the man, puzzled. "What good can we do there, when the problem is here?"

As if in answer to this question, Reverend Trask suddenly pointed to the man's shirt. The front of his white night shirt had suddenly began to darken with wet blood, and the Reverend suddenly leaned over and pulled the mans now sticky shirt front up.

A new series of deep claw marks had appeared upon his chest, and blood was trickling down the front of his shirt in lazy rivulets. Both men were too astounded to speak, and the Reverend felt, for the first time in years, a true, deep sense of spiritual danger, the likes of which was threatening to shake from him every last once of his spiritual fortitude. He said, "I have to leave, Sir. Begging your pardon, but I must insist on seeing both you and your wife in the presence of several of the brothers of our congregation. You see, I've heard of this sort of thing before, never believed I would see it first hand, though. It would be advisable to have a few others present, to assist if there is any danger."

"What are you talking about? What's going on here?" The man, suddenly, seemed to be on the verge of losing his stability. He wiped his hand across his bloody chest, stood on trembling legs, and walked from the bedroom as his wife was just coming up from below. He brushed past her, going into the bathroom and slamming the door.

"See if you can talk some sense into him. And be very careful. I would suggest you find somewhere else to stay for the time being. If you need anything, anything at all, do not hesitate to contact me. My prayers will be with you."

The wife looked as distressed as any woman he had ever seen, and he felt deeply troubled for her as he walked out the front door and shakily got into his car, driving away and not even daring to look back over his shoulder.

He felt very happy to be leaving that damnable house, too.

That evening he spent the night in fervid prayer, not breathing a word of what had happened to his own wife, but carrying the memory of that ghastly coldness and malignant evil into sleep with him.

He felt a deep sense of guilt, for he made no plans whatsoever to check back with the family. He couldn't. That small experience had shaken his faith to its very core, and as he grappled with the failure of his religion, he did his best to bury the memory as one would a bad dream. His phone remained silent, and no messages were left for him for nearly two weeks.

Then, finally, as if the terror had just been toying with him, he awoke one sober morning, his wife still laying beside him, curled up and blissfully unaware. He looked out the window at the trickle of gray, early morning rain, and knew that today would be the day.

Sure enough, when he came home for lunch, having gone calling on elderly parishioners all that morning, his wife announced that a woman had called earlier that morning, leaving a message concerning her husband's illness. He had almost managed to slip the strange sense of gloom that had settled over him all day, but now, deep inside, he felt the icy claws of alien terror seize the back of his neck. He quickly sorted through his mental Rolodex, turning over in his mind who he might be able to contact that might be of help later this evening. He then dialed the number the woman had left with trembling fingers, and stilled his nervousness when her voice finally answered on the other end.

To the surprise of Reverend Trask, the woman was currently at the hospital, her husband having been admitted due to illness and nervous exhaustion. Apparently, since last they met, the husband had become increasingly despondent and unresponsive, and had become unable to keep any food down. Doctors attributed this to a mild flu, and to the aforementioned "nervous exhaustion." The scratches they attributed to psychological disturbance, and had insisted he be hospitalized for observation.

"You mean, they think that he is doing it to himself?"

"Oh yes," the wife replied. "They think he's gone off the deep end, and they want to commit him to a sanitarium, I think."

"And what of the disturbances? Have they continued?"

She sounded a little morose when she replied. "Yes, but they seemed to settle down some, the worse he got. There were still strange footsteps, heavy breathing, and things flying through the air. Things would disappear, and you could hear clawing along the walls, same as always. We left several days ago, to stay in a hotel, and then stay with friends, but we couldn't really explain to anyone what was happening, and we couldn't really believe it ourselves. Then, day before yesterday, the scratches returned, and he started getting very ill, vomiting and crying out that something was attacking him. I...I didn't know what to do, so I called an ambulance. He's sleeping now."

"Do you think we could take him out for a little while tonight?"

She said, hesitantly: "He's very sedated, but I think he can get around. If you can convince the doctors to sign him out, I'm sure he'd go."

"If anyone can convince them, I can. Don't worry about that. I'll be there in just a short while."

He hung up the phone, and then instructed his wife to keep a plate in the oven for him. She protested mildly, but realizing the nature of his work and always trusting his judgment, she did as he asked. He went upstairs to change into a fresh suit, found his briefcase, and set out just as the sun started dipping low behind the overhanging trees in the backyard.

He first went to the home of one of his most loyal parishioners, and implored the man to meet him at the church in a quarter of an hour. The man replied that he most certainly would, and would even bring his son-in-law along. Reverend Trask then hopped back in his car and sped to the hospital.

Upon entering, he was met by the wife, who looked gravely ill from lack of sleep and sheer worry. "He's just awoken, but he's heavily doped. Follow me."

She led him to the elevator and up into the general wards. As he walked into the room, he found himself aghast at the sight he beheld. The man seemed to have literally shrunken inward since last he had seen him. He was deathly pale, had lost weight, and his haggard visage bore testament to the increasingly harrowing ordeal he had suffered over the past several weeks. Also, his arms had been bandaged to hide, the Reverend supposed, the ever accumulating wounds that seemingly appeared on this man as if in some bizarre mockery of the stigmata suffered by some pious Catholics.

He walked to the man's bedside and held out his hand. The man looked over at him groggily.

Help me, his bleary eyes seemed to implore. Reverend Trask intended to do just that.

He took the man's hand for a moment, squeezed, and then went to find a doctor. It took some convincing on the part of the Reverend, but finally the man's doctor was located at home. Although he at first seemed reluctant, there was nothing, specifically, he objected to about having his patient go out to the church for a "spiritual healing." The Reverend wasted no small amount of time in getting to the chapel, anxiously waiting for the gentleman he had already made arrangements with to come and assist. Then he solemnly took a few moments to kneel down at his desk, and solemnly prayed to his God that everything should turn out well, they should be successful, and whatever evil had managed to attach itself to this family should be driven out and depart.

When his assistant finally arrived, they talked for awhile over coffee concerning what to expect, all the while feeling a greater sense of trepidation grow in the gloom of the basement office. They all knelt, and again prayed before going upstairs, past the wall-sized mural of Jesus emerging from his tomb, which shone out in heavy colors in the shadows.

They had only waited for a few moments, when the outer door of the sanctuary opened, and in came the wife, leading her obviously-ill husband beside her as if her were an aged invalid. The man looked, in the sub-

dued light of the church sanctuary, like some impover-
ished mendicant come to offer penance. He sat down
on the front pew heavily, his eyes looking drained, and
apprehension settling on his face.

Reverend Trask stood in front of the pulpit for a moment, with his hands clasped over his Bible. His two assistants flanked him on either side, and he looked down
at the man, saying: "Well, it looks like the only thing left
to do is put it in God's hands. Do you agree?"

The man looked at him for a moment, and his eyes
seemed to reflect all the misery and torment in the
world. Then his jaw hardened into bitter resolve, and he
croaked, tearfully, "Reverend, I don't believe in God."

"So I understand. However, I think that if you stop
and consider all that has happened to you, you could
afford, for a few moments, to entertain the possibility
that there is something beyond the ability of our rational
minds to understand…"

He trailed off, and suddenly he motioned for the
man's wife to stand and move out of the way. The three
men circled him where he sat, and began to murmur
prayers, bending over and laying hands upon his
shoulders. They at first started as a general whisper,
but their voices shortly became a fervent drone, their
exhortations for mercy and intervention on behalf
of God rising in pitch as the man seated below them
began to tremble.

Suddenly, he jerked away from them, falling to the
floor and writhing as if he were having a seizure. The
men with Reverend Trask stalled for a moment, drawing back as if unsure of their own faith, or of what to do
when confronted with such a crisis. However, it was not
long before they got to the floor, holding the man's arms
down as Reverend Trask began to solemnly intone:

"In the name of Jesus Christ, the Lamb slain for the sins of the world, we command you, Satan, to leave this man and his wife alone!"

"Shut up! Shut up, you damned old fool!"

The man let loose with a string of profanities, and the men holding him were awed at the sudden immense strength he seemed to be exhibiting. It was all both of them could do to keep him from springing forward and running out the door.

The man squirmed, and one of the men holding him put his knee on his shoulder, holding him down as the Reverend continued to put his hand on the man's forehead. The man spat up a vile froth of greenish phlegm, and suddenly one of the men remarked how cold it had grown.

Indeed, suddenly, the men could see their breath blow misty in the air, and felt the freezing onrush of pure evil surround them. Reverend Trask continued his imprecations before God.

Suddenly:

"What's your name?"

"That's none of your damn business!"

Vile language erupted from the man's mouth in a hideous, deep growl that was not his own. His eyes rolled upward into his head, and a vile stink began to erupt from his body. The men realized, as they held him, that he was bleeding from a variety of puzzling wounds.

The man's wife stood crying, her hand over her mouth, her body trembling. She looked, all of a sudden, as if the pressure and oppression of the last few weeks was draining out of her at once. She seemed as if she was on the verge of collapse.

The lights in the sanctuary began to flicker, as if the power were under an incredible strain, and suddenly, the men began to hear a heavy pounding coming from downstairs. It sounded like something below, in the basement, was threatening to knock the building down.

"I command you, in the name of Jesus Christ, Son of the Most High God, to tell me your name!"

The man thrashed about again, and suddenly broke free from those holding him. He dove forward, as if he was thrust from behind, and then collapsed across the altar suddenly in exhaustion. He was gasping heavily for air.

Instantly, as if someone had fired a cannon downstairs, the men heard a loud report. The stench was now abominable, as if they were standing amid the ruins of a slaughterhouse sewer. Then, with the blowing of a gentle breeze, as if from nowhere, it dissipated.

The lights in the sanctuary ceased to flicker, and the three men drew heavy, gusty sighs. Reverend Trask went forward to look at the crumpled figure on the pulpit floor. The man before him sat up, shaking badly, looking as if he had just been ridden to the brink of madness by some sadistic fiend. But his eyes were clear, and he had no memory of how he had come to be sitting in the church, surrounded by his wife, the Reverend, and two strangers.

Also, amazingly, though his clothes were still covered in spots of blood, and the men that had been restraining him all bore evidence of bloodstains on their hands and clothing, they could find no sign whatsoever of a single mark or wound on the man's body.

His scratches had healed without leaving even a slight scar.

Reverend Trask swore his two assistants to secrecy in the matter, not wanting to cause the young couple any sort of embarrassment. Although the disturbances did return, for a short time, they were a mere pale imitation of what they had been; they were no longer severe, nor did they adversely effect the daily lives of the man and his wife. They kept their house, and raised their children there.

The man himself never again experienced strange scratches or wounds of any kind, nor did he again suffer from the heavy melancholy and bizarre fugue that had been caused, presumably, by the offending spirit that had attached itself like a parasite to his mind. He and his wife became avid churchgoers, parishioners of Reverend Trask, and ended up raising a large family in the very same house that they had once considered evil.

Martin Sheets

The story of Martin Sheets is one that has always smelled a faint whiff comical. For those of you who have never heard this venerable anecdote recounted, let me be the first to enlighten you.

Martin Sheets was an exceptionally well-off business entrepreneur that made his home in Terre Haute, Indiana. We can surmise, due to the age of the tale, that he must have made his money during the First World War, and however much money he in reality had, he was by all accounts well-enough to indulge a few strange, personal fixations.

We can also assume that, being a man of the world, he was less-than-enthusiastic about the prospects of leaving it badly. Hence, a continued obsession of his involved a morbid fantasy of being…buried alive.

In an age when embalming was not, strictly speaking, standard practice, the possibility was not very far-fetched. The oft-told tales of premature burial have been a staple of the literature of the macabre for centuries, even influencing the great Edgar Allan Poe to concoct his own tale in homage to the hideous occurrence. There *have* been instances, as in the case of a small boy in Pennsylvania who was reportedly interred after falling into a narcoleptic trance. Due to the prescient dreams of his aggrieved mother, his grave was inspected and it was found that the boy lay inside his coffin on his side, exactly as his mother had dreamed of him the night before. Upon being taken back to the house and treated medically, he fully recovered, and lived to a ripe old age.

Earlier accounts are less comforting. The dead, when disinterred to make additional space, were often seen to be clutching handfuls of hair torn from the roots, turned completely around in their caskets, as if in shock, and their nails were frequently dug into the top of the box. It was horrifying stuff, and made for a morbid topic.

The Victorian obsession with being "buried alive" grew to such outrageous proportions that a special device was marketed, wherein a supposedly deceased person, having awakened in the darkness of the grave, could pull a string and thereby ring a bell that had been attached to a pulley above ground. A sentry, left to stand guard at the graveside lest the individual beneath him should call for immediate exhumation, would then be charged to summon help—hopefully gravediggers.

What a prematurely interred individual was to do if the sentry fell asleep, failed to be aroused by the bell, or better yet, made off for a night of drinking in various and sundry pubs, is not known.

At any rate, Mr. Sheets was thoroughly and utterly consumed by this very fear, and, being an individual of some means, endeavored to put his troubled mind to rest. He set about spending his considerable wealth on the construction of a specialized tomb, the likes of which would allow him not only luxuriant rest for all of eternity, but would also ensure that, were he not quite ready yet to be shut of this world in a medical sense, he could quite easily free himself from the constraints of his expensive coffin and wait for help to arrive.

How was he to summon help? the cautious reader asks himself. As Shakespeare would say, "therein lays the rub." Mr. Sheets became, perhaps, the only man in America during his era to have his tomb equipped not only with food and wine, a comfortable couch, and an opening casket, but also with that most mysterious of all new-fangled inventions: the telephone.

Invented in 1877 by Alexander Graham Bell, the telephone is the most commonplace and recognizable of all modern technological innovations. It has served an indispensable use for over a century, and is as ingrained into the consciousness of every man, woman, and child alive as the automobile or the airplane.

So let us establish, here and now, that there is nothing sinister about a telephone, no matter where it happens to be installed, or for what purpose.

Mr. Sheets, having laid his mind to easy rest, quickly overcame his debilitating fear of death and burial, and quickly set about the business of making more money. That he was successful in this we can take for granted, if only because the story never makes quite clear about the exact circumstances of his life during his later years.

However, as sure as Winter follows Fall, Mr. Sheets, having toiled long upon this Earth, and having reaped from it all the pleasure and prosperity any one man could hope for in the course of his existence, suffered a severe and debilitating physical attack and expired shortly after. It may have been heart attack, stroke, or some other sudden, life-threatening malady, but what-ever it was, Mr. Sheets was flung rather unceremoniously forward into that "undiscovered country, from whence once borne no traveler returns."

On the other hand, was he?

The doctor, at the very least, was sure that Mr. Sheets was dead. Pulse and respiratory function had ceased, and there was no heartbeat. The flesh was cold to the touch, of an unhealthy pallor, and rigor mortis was soon going to claim the body and render it little more than a stiff, immobile puppet of slowly putrefying flesh.

In short, Mr. Sheets was ready to lay down his withered head on the soft , frilly lace lining of his personal shroud, and repose there in quiet earnest, forevermore.

Arrangements were hastily made, and no expense was spared to see the great man off in style. We may assume there was a funeral procession, as vast as a parade and as lofty as anything death-related that had yet been seen on the streets of Terre Haute, Indiana. Locals milled about and reminisced, some of them not kindly, about Mr. Sheets, and not a few in the know tittered about the eccentric man's macabre obsession.

Martin Sheets was laid to rest and his widow escorted home, not much worse for her ordeal, to embark upon a solitary life spent with a few trusted friends, a photo album of fading images, and memories.

However, it was not to be a bed of roses and relaxation for Mrs. Sheets. Quite the contrary: For after a short time, the elderly woman began to show the signs of an early, creeping senility.

She wandered the house, sitting up at all hours, insisting she could hear the footsteps of her husband as they clicked up the cement sidewalk, or tottered around in his disused upstairs office. At one point, she told her daughter that she could have sworn, as she lay in the darkness of her room one evening that Martin had come in from the back hallway and had walked, with slow, deliberate steps, down the hall. He had even tested the doorknob, as she trembled with terror and wonder. When asked if she thought the noises might, instead, be coming from an intruder or burglar, she replied, almost as if in relief: "Heavens no! Why, I lived with the man for forty years. I know his sounds, his own peculiar walk and step, his breathing, and I could smell the heavy scent of his tobacco. You remember the way it clung to his clothing like a shroud."

Perhaps her choice of words was poor. However, her daughter and her husband, both very fond of the elderly Mrs. Sheets, resolved that they should stay with her for awhile, her only company being an elderly housekeeper that left during the evening. They suggested, initially, hiring a nurse, but Mrs. Sheets wouldn't hear of it. She was far too young yet, she assured them, to have to be bothered with constant medical supervision.

Mrs. Sheets daughter was grimly determined, however, to keep a wary eye on her widowed mother, and in short order had moved herself and her husband in with their lonely mother, as much to keep a eye on her as to assure themselves that they were truly doing everything in their power to assure the safety and security of Mrs. Sheets.

For a short period, perhaps a happy period, life seemed to return to normal. The Sheets family (what was left of it, at any rate) lived under the creaking floorboards and groaning timbers of the old place, keeping careful watch over the elderly mother, and making sure as to keep their guard in any event, for the return of the presumed intruder. Life puttered back into a sense of normality, and for a short while, seemed as if it might pick up and proceed as it always had.

Then one day, Mrs. Sheets' daughter informed her mother that, regrettably, her husband was being called away for a few days on business, and that she intended to join him on the trip. Although initially Mrs. Sheets was disturbed at the thought of being left alone, she suddenly had a change of heart, and a smile crept across her wizened features, as she stated, calmly: "You go right ahead and enjoy yourself, dear. I'll be fine."

In a few days they were gone, but the daughter found it increasingly difficult to forget herself in the excitement of travel, at last becoming despondent one night while staying in a hotel room.

She had started crying, begging her husband to let them both return home early, to make sure her mother was still all right. He thought her silly at first, but a creeping unease had started to settle over him as well, and he hastily went downstairs to the lobby to telephone home.

To his amazement, he was unable to reach her, and deciding that there could be little time to waste, he dialed a family friend and requested that the man walk on over to the Sheets residence, and make sure everything was still as it should be.

He then went back upstairs and told his wife what he had done, lighting his cigar and sitting down for a few moments before he went downstairs to see if his friend had called back to leave a message.

It was just as well that neither of them had been there in person. The gentleman who had been drafted into checking up on the elderly Mrs. Sheets had left his home with a walking stick and a whistle, had proceeded down the sidewalk, through the gate, across the yard, and up the old porch until he came to the darkened doorway of the residence. He tapped lightly with his cane, more fiercely with his hand, and then rather loudly with his closed fist.

Unable to rouse the woman, he rather shamefully crept behind the hedge to look through the front room window at the parlor. He strained his eyes, peering into the darkness.

He could make out what appeared to be a figure dressed in filmy white, lying halfway across the floor, clutching something. Although he immediately shot out from the shrubs and across the yard, he did not need a second glance to tell him whose dead body had been lying alone in the darkness.

It was not long before the police made their calling, and upon investigation, indeed found the body of Mrs. Sheets lying sprawled upon the carpet. The cause of death, presumably, was natural causes, but the police officers themselves could not help but notice the terror-stricken visage that had stretched the face into a macabre grimace.

Worse, it took them several unsuccessful minutes to pry the cold, dead fingers away from the smooth surface of the telephone receiver, so tightly had the woman grasped the object upon her sudden death.

Mrs. Sheet's daughter and her husband returned a few hours later, exhausted but already prepared for the worst. The man that had initially discovered the body had been so shaken that he had completely forgotten about calling back to the hotel. Perhaps he was simply too anxious about being the bearer of horrible news.

The inquest determined cause of death to be due to coronary arrest, possibly the result of severe shock. Most assumed that Mrs. Sheets had been trying to call for help when the incipient pain in her chest started, and had simply collapsed before she was even able to dial.

Of course, in every small town or village tongues will wag, and Terre Haute at this time was no exception. Folks found the circumstances of Mrs. Sheets death to be curious, and some recalled that Mr. Sheets, having been reputedly plagued with nightmares (according to his physician's secretary, who related this little-known bit of trivia to her bridge club, under strict orders of confidentiality), had specified certain odd arrangements be made upon his internment. What those arrangements were, and what part they played in the death of the wife, decent people could only speculate.

A memorial service was held, and the funeral procession made its bleak way out to the cemetery to open the Sheets mausoleum one last time.

When the doors were opened, and the musty balm of closed crypts finally abated, the funeral party made its way into the sanctuary that was to be the resting place for husband and wife, forevermore.

Those in the know concerning the circumstances of Mrs. Sheets death then found themselves mysteriously taken aback. We might even venture to say they were greatly disturbed about the condition of the mausoleum, as it had been left intact, locked securely, and been undisturbed in the long space of time between the internment of Mr. Sheets, and the internment of his wife.

Some now saw a blackly humorous happenstance in the way things had worked out. Others, more darkly, thought of a supernatural explanation, and slept less soundly that night because of it.

For it was a telephone that Mrs. Sheets had clutched close to her bosom when she died, and it was the telephone that had been absurdly installed in the Sheets mausoleum that so consternated the assembled mourners as they gawped in wonder at their discovery. Somehow, locked in a vault with only a dead man as close company, the receiver had been taken off the hook.

Belle Gunness

Belle Gunness was a lady fair,
From Indiana State;
She weighed about three hundred pounds,
And that is quite some weight.

—Traditional Folk Ballad

The story of Belle Gunness is one that is familiar to the great majority of true-crime enthusiasts who are forever in search of some classic atrocity to ruminate and obsess over. A short recounting of the Belle Gunness mystery will serve to enlighten those not privileged to have ever heard it before.

Belle Gunness was a large, homely spinster of Norwegian ancestry who made her living by advertising in "lonely hearts" columns for marriageable men desperate to settle down with a friendly, accommodating woman.

Belle, who was stout, flat-faced, and had roughly the build of a small professional wrestler, may not have quite been what these individuals had in mind.

It was a small matter, though, if Belle's physical graces did not live up to the expectations of those luckless souls who came to call on her at her hog farm in La Porte. These gentlemen would not, after all, be around long enough to tire of the homely visage and gray demeanor of their sordid paramour. The would-be lovers seldom lived to see the next sunrise.

Belle, who many regard as America's first legitimate

female serial killer (Aileen Wuornous notwithstanding) began her grisly endeavors in 1908. Her first victim was, quite possibly, her husband Peter Gunness. After toiling one day at butchering hogs, an enormous meat grinder slipped from a shelf and pulverized his skull. The local coroner cried "foul play!" but it did little good: Belle was exonerated by an incredulous jury of any wrongdoing in her husband's death.

Having now at her disposal a relatively large, private area in which to ply her strange new trade, she wasted no time in securing the services of a local alcoholic handyman to both maintain the farm and tend to whatever other additional responsibilities as might be required of him.

The other area of responsibility entrusted to Mr. Lamphere was far more sordid: He was to be the masculine half of the Belle Gunness Lonely Hearts Club Killers, and it was a role he took to as easily as tossing back cheap hooch or slopping hogs.

The eventual number of murdered men who made the unfortunate mistake of traveling to the Gunness farm in search of a spouse is estimated to be around fourteen. The Modus Operendi, which was in effect up until the very end of the sorry saga, had Belle running out of the house to greet her new beau. He would, presumably, be less-than-enthusiastic upon first catching sight of her, but would remain as tolerably polite as was possible under the circumstances. Joe Lamphere, the drunken handyman, would then strut from the house and out onto the porch, peeling an apple and looking pensive. Belle would offer apologies to the jilted suitor, telling him that Belle had decided that Joe Lamphere was the love of her life, and that she was deeply regretful for having the gentleman come all the way to Laporte just to be told his romantic interest was marrying someone else.

Although in many cases, this may have actually relieved the man in question rather than infuriated him, Belle nonetheless continued with the contrite charm, inviting the man to dinner and a nap before he set out again to return home still a bachelor.

The man, typically thankful for just a short respite from the backbreaking travel, readily assented, and in coming inside the home was greeted with a sizeable table full of sumptuous home cooking.

As he bit into the roasted pork, or savored the potatoes, he would in short order notice a rather strange, bitter undertaste that, while not seriously impinging upon the enjoyment of the dinner, did grow substantially less tolerable as the meal progressed. Later, perhaps reclining in a chair having an after-dinner smoke, he would begin to feel dizzy and "not quite right." He would then fall into a deep swoon, from which he would not awake.

It was Joe Lamphere who handled the really dirty business of crushing the heads and dismembering the bodies. Whatever money and possessions as could be found on the individual's person were soon rifled, and became the property of Mrs. Gunness. Later, Joe could offer fresh meat to hungry hogs, the swine grown spoiled from such delectably fresh vittles.

Of course, there were times when the M. O. was slightly altered. Belle seemed to have a nose for money, and when she hooked a fresh prospect, she was willing to string him along a bit, so as to reap as much financial benefit as she could. Often, she would write in advance, letting each besotted male know that she was, badly, in need of money. Sums of up to one thousand dollars were, according to later testimony, sent to Belle, from men who sincerely thought they had finally found the answer to their long, lonely existence.

The most troubling, astonishing thing was the fact that while Belle was busily engaged in this bloody undertaking, she also managed to rear three children, all of whom were apparently oblivious to the goings-on in their own home. They would each share the same unhappy fate.

All went along fairly well for Belle, until finally she happened upon a prospect the likes of which would come back to seal her fate. It was a man named Hegelian who presented himself at the Gunness residence as the final suitor. He too disappeared in a small amount of time. However, unlike the preceding victims, he had relatives who knew where he had been headed, and were concerned not to hear from him. In time, his own brother began to hunt for him, and the trail led him to Belle Gunness' front door.

A fire gutted the Gunness residence shortly after, and it was assumed by the town folk of La Porte, as well as the esteemed Sheriff Smutzer, that Belle had perished therein, along with her three children. Joe Lamphere, who was immediately arrested under suspicion of arson, confessed to a string of horrors too bizarre for the imaginations of the law enforcement officers who sat spellbound, as he talked through the night.

One thing was for certain, he made clear to them: Belle Gunness was not dead, but her children were. The body that was moldering in the morgue belonged not to Belle Gunness, but to a prostitute from Chicago whom Belle had lured to her home under the pretence of a lesbian attraction. As for Belle, she had promised to come and be off with him after the fire was set and the evidence destroyed. Evidently, she had not been faithful to the luckless Lamphere, and so he would swing in her stead.

Indeed, it took only a short examination to determine that the badly burned corpse was not that of the short, stout Belle. It was too tall, and not of sufficient weight. However, what must have interested the police more than the obvious substitution of a single corpse, was the small cemetery of bodies and pieces of bodies they later unearthed from her property.

And what of Belle? She disappears into the fabric of criminal lore. Some had her as a whorehouse madam in Chicago; others suggested she had left for California, or sighted her as far away as Paris. As to her earthly whereabouts and remains, we can only hazard a guess.

However, citizens of La Porte will swear, against all logic, that the spirit of Belle Gunness has returned to her former property, perhaps to keep a matronly eye on the development and use of her blood-soaked soil.

The house that now stands where once Belle butchered men has its own bizarre goings-on, with freak electrical occurrences, televisions and computers that turn on and off by themselves, strange creaking footsteps, and phantasmal "friends" that like to keep company with small children. Workmen recently contracted to remodel after a freak fire, reported eerie feelings, chilling coldspots, levitating ladders, and objects that would vanish, only to reappear in the most bizarre of places.

But the most astonishing reports come from those who have driven along dark McClung road, and seen standing in the light of a full moon the figure of a large, menacing woman dressed in old fashioned garb, waiting like a lost soul in the shifting shadows.

Some accounts speak of the frightening phantom chasing them, or of the sickening scream of a murdered man sounding out across the fields in the darkness. Some say the black garbed woman cackles maniacally in the night, still gleeful at the ease with which she made her escape after killing so many men.

Some say these things, and some may even believe them. As to the objective truth concerning Belle Gunness and her ghost, no one knows for certain.

Stepp Cemetery

Tourists along the spectral back roads of haunted Indiana will do well to stop, for a brief repose, at fabled Stepp Cemetary, or "One Hundred Step Cemetery," in Terre Haute.

Local legend describes the eerie cemetery as being the abode of the ghost of the very first undertaker, who died in the late nineteenth century.

On the grassy hill leading up to the oldest area of the cemetery are one hundred stone steps. The enlightened visitor is encouraged to walk these stone steps upward, careful to count each one as he goes. Then, when he is to the top, he should be certain to turn and face the open field. Legend has it that it is then that the ghost of the first undertaker will appear, as a misty wraith in the moonlight, and will then proceed to show the curious climber a vision of his impending death.

When the curious soul has thus been shown how he is to die, he is then supposed to walk carefully back down the old stone steps in the side of the hill, counting as he goes.

If, upon reaching the bottom, he counts to one hundred, the vision is assumed to be wrong, and the individual can go about his way, secure in the knowledge that death is still a long way off.

However, if he fails to count one hundred steps on the way down, then that person is doomed to suffer the sorry fate shown to him in the macabre vision of the cemetery ghost.

One can only suppose how such a morbid tale got started. Perhaps it was the folly of a solitary youth, or even a gang of youths, each daring the other to take the night time walk up the ancient steps to the top. Perhaps imagination supplied whatever ghost was conjured that dark, forlorn night so long ago.

And if one of them on the way down happened to miss a step, miscount, or in some other way come to a number less than one hundred, and if this same individual, by happenstance, came to meet a tragic, unexpected end…You can well see how such a grotesque little tale might have started.

It is no good taking the hill up without climbing the stairs, for then, it is said, a horrid creature of darkness, a foul demon from the pits of Hell, will grab the unsuspecting transgressor and hurl him backward with a mighty push. The person or persons will then find that they have had their skin imprinted forever with a hideous red brand, a sort of hooked claw that is the mark of the Devil. Or so the legend goes.

Other visitors to One Hundred Step Cemetery relate a tale of a mysterious weeping woman, seen to spend her time scouring the ancient grounds, or sitting in mournful repose upon the lid of an ancient tomb, weeping for her lost love.

Who she is, or rather was, none can specifically say, but a number of reliable witnesses claim that here is where she makes her home: Lost in an afterlife of undying grief; weeping for, perhaps, her baby that died at birth.

Stepp Cemetery is also reputedly a center for "Satanic Ritual Practices," and locals will claim that the evidence of black magic rituals and pagan practices by the living add to the awesome, lurking fear generated by the venerable old burying ground. One anonymous individual advised this writer that I should bring a gun with me if I intended to explore.

If Satanists or witches find the legendary bone yard to be homey, it is small wonder: It was once, reputedly, the favored ground of a little-known religious sect known as the Crabbites, after their maniacal leader, Jethro Crabb.

The Crabbites were a cult who, much like many of their contemporaries, preached a bizarre combination of Christianity and occult beliefs. Supposedly they were involved in bizarre, orgiastic rites that horrified their respectable straight-laced neighbors. Shunned and despised among their more orthodox religious neighbors, they claimed Stepp Cemetery as a sanctuary, a place where they could be free from the constraints of rural American mores and commune with each other—and with the dead, we must presume—in any manner they liked.

But the Crabbites disappeared, fading into the history of the region like a phantom shadow before the rays of daybreak.

However, if you should find yourself in Terre Haute, and wish to kill a few hours investigating the veracity of a very odd tale, try your hand at climbing the One Hundred Steps.

Just remember: Make sure you keep your count exactly on the way down, lest you become a restless resident of Stepp Cemetery.

The Nursing Home Haunt

My mother doesn't like the supernatural; in fact, it pretty much scares her silly. So when she tells me a real-life ghost story, I tend to prick up my ears and pay attention.

After all, it isn't as if she spends her spare time collecting these anecdotes because she likes them. That's my special provenance. But I digress.

As a child, while I was spending my spare time encountering spirits aplenty in my bedroom, and in the open fields of childhood play, my mother worked as a nurse's aid at a nursing home in our small Indiana town of Marion. As anyone that has ever worked in the healthcare profession can tell you, death is a common visitor-in-wait at such institutions. The elderly live out the remainder of their lives staving it off to the last, and when they go, it is usually in the privacy of their own beds, while sleeping.

My mother, during her first few weeks of work at this particular institution, learned that a certain couple had recently been separated by the death of the husband, a man whose devotion to his wife was as profound as hers to him. Although the couple had lived together happily in the nursing home for several years, ill-health had left both of them burdened in the last years, and with the death of the husband, it was not long before the wife deteriorated to the point where she had to be moved to another ward where she could be more carefully watched over.

It was only a day or two after that the wife was transferred to an entirely different institution, and the couple's personal belongings were left behind, awaiting the family to come and claim them. It was at this time that the situation took a strange, eerie turn.

Upon entering the room one morning, one of the housekeepers found that the place had been, quite literally, torn apart: Drawers had been ripped out of the dresser, their contents spilled to the floor and cast aside. The covers had been torn from the bed, chairs were tipped over, old photographs had been thrown about, and it generally looked as if someone had come in and had a very nasty tantrum in the middle of the night. Of course, no one had ever heard a thing.

Since the police could find no signs of forced entry, and the closed-circuit surveillance cameras had not recorded the entrance of anyone into the nursing home during the night, the staff remained puzzled, but generally tried to maintain an aura of calm about the incident.

It was later that evening that my mother, while making her final rounds for the evening, was walking down the corridor outside the room where the old couple had lived. She noticed what appeared to be a stooped, wheezing old man walking with a cane down the hallway.

Wondering why the old man wasn't in his room sleeping, she approached him, and was amazed, as she turned the corridor to follow him, to find that he had seemingly disappeared without a trace.

She wiped her eyes, trying to put the occurrence down to fatigue, but it disturbed her so greatly that the next day, in the employee break room, she related her experience to her co-workers, and upon describing the old man, was met with some seemingly startled assertions that the description fit the old man that had just died.

My mother, who had just started working at the place, had no idea what the man looked like, but she was able to describe him to her senior co-workers exactly, and the realization soon grew that the restless spirit of the old man had not moved off the premises after he shuffled off his body.

As if to verify this, several hours later, when the errant family finally showed to claim the items left behind by their elderly parents, the room was once again opened, and the scene inside was shocking: Chairs overturned, bedding ripped to shreds, walls clawed as if by manic fingers, picture frames broken, and old items pounded to general rubble, They littered the floor and created amazement.

This was a vandalism that the nursing home had never before witnessed, and as before, the police could find no sign of an intruder. It was as if an invisible man had snuck in, walked through the locked door of the room, and exploded into rage.

The family claimed what few objects they could manage to salvage, but it was after this that the strange noises began.

It was the wheezy, tear-choked voice of an old man, calling out in barely-discernible speech, and it got to a point where employees started refusing to work along that particular lonely corridor near the late man's room at night.

Finally, fed up to the teeth with the weird goings-on, the administration of the nursing home at last decided to bring in an expert: A Spiritualist who specialized in dealing with the deceased when they have lost their way.

Since our hometown is not forty-five minutes away from the celebrated Camp Chesterfield, the hub of American Spiritualism in the Midwest, it was not difficult to locate an individual who was thoroughly experienced with just such a disturbance. The medium quickly ascertained what was troubling the ghost, and assured the administration of the home that it amounted to his confusion concerning the whereabouts of his wife.

So how was the situation finally dealt with? Not, as might be expected, with an exorcism or even a "spirit rescue," but in a far more conventional manner.

They simply wrote the ghost a polite letter, stating:

> "Sir. Your wife has been moved to a different location. Could you kindly move on as well? Thank you. —The Staff."

And, unbelievably, this approach worked, and their were no more disturbances. At the very least, not from that particular spirit.

Much to the relief of my mother.

Unhallowed Hills and Happy Haunts: A Tour

Although requirements of length forbid us from examining every conceivable haunted nook and cranny of the Hoosier State (must save something for the sequel, after all), we feel justifiably certain that we can, succinctly, offer you a quick, "haunted tour" of some back road phantasms that are not to be missed by any wanderer of the spectral vale.

Peru

So climb aboard our rickety wagon, pull your jacket around your shoulders, and suppress a shiver, because we're going to take a midnight ride on the Devil's own coach through a half-dozen or more unhallowed hills and happy haunting grounds.

Our first stop takes us to Peru, where the mystery of an unearthed skeleton, discovered on the property of Jacob Rife, still haunts the local townspeople.

In 1927, while digging in the old gravel pit on the banks of the Wabash, workers uncovered the grisly spectacle of long-dead remains, hunched into a sitting posture, and buried—presumably—alive. Although an official enquiry was launched, the identity of the man was never uncovered, and in time, the bizarre artifact was transferred to the ownership of the Miami County Historical Society. Today, the unknown corpse rests as a curio in the Miami County Museum, an illustrious finale to a rather inauspicious end.

However, those that comb the banks of the Wabash River area at night looking for a spectral hint of a solution to the mystery won't find themselves disappointed, for it is said that on certain nights, a weird clammy mist hangs to the ground, and brilliant glowing orbs of light can be see floating over the ground, while the strange wailing of a maniacal man is heard calling out in the darkness with imprecations of pity, and demands for justice.

Bloomington

Next, we turn our phantom coach toward Bloomington, where Indiana University and McNutt Quad is located, in search of the inimitably named "Hatchet Man," a deviant sex-predator who committed a string of grisly homicides decades ago. The legend concerning the nefarious Hatchet Man (whom, you may have guessed by now, was never apprehended) involves two college co-eds who, not mindful of the warning to stay inside at night while the hunt was on for the maniac, skipped out for an evening on the town. When one of the girls became tired early, she decided to head home by herself. On the way, she thought she heard footsteps close by, and becoming frightened, ran into her dormitory room as fast as she could, slamming the door behind her. Although worried about her friend, she quickly fell asleep, not stirring to wakefulness until the first few beams of sunshine began to filter through the window drapes.

Upon awakening, she noticed with a mounting sense of trepidation that her roommate's bed had not been slept in. As she went to the door, she realized that a thin, trickling red was spilling in from outside, as if someone had made a mess with a drink outside their door.

She opened the door, and as her mind reeled into shock, her scream pierced the early morning stillness of the dormitory as she bolted over the mutilated corpse of her friend and ran screaming down the hall.

It was, undoubtedly, the work of the Hatchet Man, and the body had been cut in a far more grisly fashion than any of his preceding victims. A pool of drying blood pasted the limp body of the young girl to the hallway floor, and upon removing the corpse, investigators noticed that the girl had dug her fingers into the wood in a frenzied attempt to rouse her sleeping friend. There were great, jagged claw marks defacing the surface.

To this day, it is said that the heavy tread of an invisible man can be heard stalking through the corridors, followed by bizarre scratching and the horrified screams of a murdered girl.

Vevay

Next we come into pleasant Vevay, in Switzerland County, and make a stop at the mansion of Benjamin Franklin Schenk, a local business magnate who built the ornate structure as an American palace.

Its gaudy architecture and massive bulk enclosed a house as elegant as its exterior. Sadly, the prosperous owner was only allowed to enjoy his castle for a short time, dying only three years after its construction. His daughter then donated the unwieldy edifice to the local citizens of Vevay, and the house was turned, after a few years, into an orphanage. Many decades later, the crumbling Schenk Mansion was only a shadow of its former glory, when a local man purchased the dwelling in hopes of establishing a hotel.

However, finding workmen to assist in the renovation proved to be difficult, as the home bore the tell-tale signs of having succumbed through the years to more than dust and dry rot.

The house was haunted by the presence of a tall, matronly woman, dressed in white, who played havoc with the workmen, sabotaging their efforts and doing her level best to make a mischievous nuisance of herself.

The restoration effort proceeded despite her best efforts, but the owner swears to having glimpsed the presence of this phantom Victorian woman walking stoically through the halls at odd hours, and has even described strange "petting" and "kisses" emanating from the ghost. On a fitful night, he relates, she may deign to crawl into bed next to him, an icy reminder that what lies beneath the dust of time is not always apt to stay put.

Terre Haute

Of course, spectral ladies are nothing at all new: Stepp Cemetery, whose history we have already recounted, is home to a famous " Lady in Black," who bewails the loss of her daughter in a car accident. She is usually seated, when she appears, on a massive tree trunk carved into a sort of "Warlock Throne" (as it has become popularly known; it is alternately called the "Witch's Seat"). She is said, at times, to bear a heavy chain around her foot, and has even been seen carrying the decapitated head of her daughter, a luckless flapper who was killed in an automobile accident spurred on by her panic to be home before curfew.

Indianapolis

The site of the former Skiles Mansion in Indianapolis is also a haven of ghostly habitation. The eccentric Mr. Skiles Test, a prominent local businessman of vast wealth and means, built for himself and his extended family a lavish estate fully equipped with its own electric power plant and water reserve. Mr. Test, very fond of animals, fostered an entire menagerie, performed pet funerals, and maintained his own pet cemetery. After his death, it was discovered that a series of tunnels beneath his property housed a survivalist's treasure trove of rations, fuel, water, and other amenities conducive to surviving an atomic holocaust. No one could ever accuse Mr. Test of not being, at all times, thoroughly prepared for disaster.

One disaster he had not foreseen, however, was the death of his beloved wife in his home, due to a faulty banister railing. Grief stricken, Mr. Test (already known for his holiday light displays) shined bizarre blue lights during that Christmas, instead of more festive red and green ones, much to the puzzlement of his neighbors. Gossip said that he was performing a bizarre spiritualistic séance involving blue lights, his wife's corpse, and a glass coffin, but no one was ever completely sure.

After his passing, the property was turned over to the city, and the house stood vacant for a time, becoming the stuff of local legend. One piece of folklore stated that to go to the door and ring the bell meant having it answered by the late Mrs. Test!

Of course, in reality, the strangest thing about the vacant lot where once stood the Skiles Test Mansion was the persistence of the strange blue lights that shine still, without bulb, electricity, or Mr. Skiles Test apparently controlling them.

These ghostly lights have been reported many times.

Hammond

Onward we go to Hammond, for a romantic rendezvous with the "Lady in White," a disembodied personage said to have given blasphemous birth in a little folkloric ditty that goes something like this:

The Lady in White was the love of a strong, brutal man who was obsessively jealous of her every move. When, after a time, he began to suspect her of having an affair, he killed her in a heat of passion, disposing of the body after nightfall in a cemetery.

A short while later, residents of Hammond were astounded by the appearance of a woman dressed in white entering a local shop, taking a bottle of milk, and walking out without paying. This happened twice, and each time she was pursued, she seemed to simply vanish while turning a corner.

Well, the third time she put in an appearance to thieve milk, three burly men followed her hastily out of the store, down the street, and all the way to the gates of the local cemetery, where she is said to have dematerialized into the mouth of a freshly-dug grave. The astounded men wasted no time in securing the services of a local gravedigger, and made posthaste to exhume whatever lay buried beneath.

They found a reeking cadaver, yet a cadaver that, though decay had set its mark upon the features, was still recognizably the Lady in White whom they had followed from the shop. Astounded, they dug further, coming to two empty milk bottles, and one fresh one. Their last discovery, though, was the most astounding.

A baby had been buried in the grave too; unlike its unfortunate mother, however, the terrified wail of the unearthed infant told the men that this baby was, amazingly, alive.

Tuckaway

Our delving into the Discorporate and their doings in the Hoosier state would not be complete without a little side trip to Tuckaway, a place built in 1907, and occupied for years by Indianapolis socialites George and Nellie Meier. Besides being very well-off financially (George was a fashion designer for L. S. Ayers), they hosted countless soirees featuring notable historical personages such as Albert Einstein, Walt Disney, George Gershwin, Mary Pickford, and Douglas Fairbanks Jr., just to name a few.

Nellie Maier, when not dabbling in art collecting, spent her spare time reading fortunes, and was reputedly quite good. It is claimed by some that she foretold the death of Carole Lombard, the wife of Clark Gable, and wasted no time in warning the actress to exercise great caution. Alas, this bit of information did nothing at all to forestall the grim tragedy that later took the life of the actress on January 15, 1942.

Of course, death waits for no one, and soon the house had changed hands. The next owner was Nellie's niece, who reputedly sold the dwelling to Kenneth Keene in 1972.

Keene reputedly believes that the ghost of Nellie's niece appeared to him, and exercised charitable warmth during a time of deep emotional crisis. Whether or not this be true, what is undoubtedly apparent in the grave goings on at Tuckaway is the persistent presence of George and Nellie, long-dead, but still gussied up and ready to entertain guests.

Visitors report strange footsteps, the smell of perfume, the opening and closing of doors, and the moving about of furniture, as well as puzzling electrical effects. Lights dim, mysteriously; television sets and radios are snapped on and off by invisible hands.

Tucked in amongst a haven of thick trees, Tuckaway is listed on the National Register of Historic Places. You may want to drop by for a visit; George and Nellie will be waiting.

McCordsville

Of course, our tour so far has taken us largely into the realm of the "High Society" portion of the hereafter: There is a grimmer, darker tale to be told of olden times; a dark chapter of prohibition gangsters like John Dillinger, who once got their nefarious jollies at The Plantation Club in McCordsville, a combination speakeasy and brothel that serviced underworld hooligans, cutthroats, creeps, and criminals of discriminating taste.

Today, the once boisterous bar and brothel that serviced the likes of Al Capone and Machine Gun Kelly is a family restaurant with a kitsch décor, playing up its reputation of old time vice with pictures of famous hoods and period furnishings. An addition is the strange spectacle of a grim lady dressed in a blue gown wandering the grounds. Said to be the ghost of a nameless prostitute, the legend has her killed by a perverted customer one night in one of the cabins on the property. She has been seen for years as an enigmatic presence.

Or so the legend goes. At any rate, The Plantation Club is known, now, as Casio's Restaurant and Lounge. We know nothing of the menu.

White River Tunnel

Everyone knows the low, mournful wail of a passing train in the night; it's a sort of primal music of the soul, a sound as inseparable from the psyche of post-Industrial mankind as the revving of an automobile engine, the static of radio, or the megalithic thump of heavy metal machinery.

The locomotive created America from the bottom up, bringing far-flung settlers closer to thriving cities, and cutting a swath through primitive lands that had never known the clacking ambience of the great iron monster before.

It is little wonder then that our next terrible tale involves a detour through the yawning, darkened mouth of a cavern that cuts its way in a slight curve through the side of a hill overlooking the White River. Built in 1857, this particular portal was, in those primitive days, watched over by a signal man, whose job it was to stay at his post, always on the lookout for the next approaching train.

When he heard its rattling clack down the length of rail, and saw the familiar puff of smoke from the rusty chimney, he would rush into the mouth of the tunnel, making sure the track was clear and unimpeded by any fallen debris. For, in those primitive times, the tunnel was a precarious construction, having nothing to support the inside of it to keep it from discharging stones and chunks of debris onto the rails.

Of course, if he found something, he would have to clear off the tracks in a hurry, and then hope he could make it out of the way of the oncoming train in time. If the debris was too much for him, or if the train was far too close to stop, he would have to signal with his lanterns and hope that the conductor would see him. Oftentimes, this became a life and death race through the tunnel with a speeding locomotive.

The ghost of White River Tunnel was an unfortunate watchman who lost the race. Frantically trying to outrun the train, he tripped and was unceremoniously separated from his head, probably with not a little agony on the part of the engineer, who by now must have been aware that his train had just killed a man. To this very day, that lonely spectre is said to walk the black mouth of the tunnel, his lantern in one hand, his bloody noggin resting in the other.

Of course, such an ancient hill and such an old railroad passage has seen more than one death, as countless accounts of murdered vagrants, butchered railroad men, and the massacre of a group of Confederate terrorists on the slope of the hill above, will attest too. Some say that, when walking through the disused tunnel, at a certain point, vague footfalls can be heard, and the strange swinging arc of old lanterns can be seen bobbing in the blackness.

Shoreline of Lake Michigan

Chugging right along, we make our next startling stop, on the shoreline of Lake Michigan, to keep a pressing appointment with the apparition of one Alice Mable Gray, who in her day became a sort of local legend. She was a mysterious woman, known for striding about the Indiana Dunes during the day completely nude, a hauntingly erotic reminder of the Amazonian power of the primal woman. In time, she became "Diana," a reference to the Roman goddess of hunting. Locals began to whisper her name more frequently, and she attracted a throng of eager male admirers, each vying jealously for a glimpse of the fabled beauty in the buff. Most were disappointed, but in time they did ascertain that she had turned her back on society, to come to the shore of Lake Michigan and inhabit a little fisherman's shack.

She was, in fact, a university graduate who hailed from a rather well-off background; she had apparently decided, upon graduation and after a short time toiling in the rat race, that the rewards of civilization were not all they were cracked up to be. She had come alone to the most secluded place she could find, in an attempt to escape it all.

Of course, a woman such as this in 1926 was just asking for attention and gossip, and she got it aplenty. One saving grace seemed to be the new man that came into her life shortly after, the heavy, brutish, scowling Paul Wilson, whom she loved for some unfathomable reason. Paul soon became her protector, although, as you will see, she surely could have done no worse had she entrusted her safety to her worst enemy.

Paul, it has been claimed, was a seedy, untrustworthy, even criminal young man with a brooding temper and a fiercely hostile nature. In a small amount of time, he had chased away what suitors and curiosity seekers remained, and settled down with his new, common-law bride in a stark, reclusive domesticity. Paul was known locally as the man you didn't want to cross.

As if to prove this, sometime later a body was found on the beach. Badly charred, it appeared as if the man had been strangled and his body set alight to badly mask the evidence. All eyes pointed to the insanely jealous Paul Wilson, but lack of evidence forbid any charges from being brought against him.

As if fleeing from suspicion, the couple found themselves in Michigan City, barely scraping together an existence, but it would all end badly, nonetheless. Alice died in complications resulting from childbirth, while the baby was, apparently, born dead as well. It is suspected that complications arose from the years of domestic abuse she suffered at the hands of Paul Wilson.

But death did not still her pulse of existence, nor did it assuage interest in her memory. Today, an annual festival is held in the area around Lake Michigan, called "Diana of the Dunes" in her honor. However, it is not simply a yearly celebration which keeps the memory of Alice Gray alive.

She has been sighted by more than one reputable witness while swimming naked in the lake, and also while walking naked in the silvery moonlight; her ghost seems to have returned here, to the once beloved dunes that seemed, during her life, to promise an escape from the cares of the modern world. Let's pray that her spirit finds in death what her body could not find while she yet lived, and strode these sandy beaches in search of inner peace.

French Lick

From the sandy shores of Lake Michigan, to the unhallowed halls of the French Lick Hotel, our journey through the darkness of haunted Indiana is taking a detour through the black backways of history to meet a man known for his association with a mysterious secret society that formulated in post-Civil War Era America: The Knights of the Golden Circle.

The French Lick Hotel was first constructed, in the years leading up to the Civil War, by an enterprising Southerner named Dr. Bowles. An ornate and costly structure, it quickly established itself as a cultural center of French Lick—a town that, during the conflagration years of brother killing brother, showed its true nature and humanitarian spirit by establishing itself as a crucial outpost along the "Underground Railroad" to freedom.

Dr. Bowles, though living in Indiana, was still a Southern gentleman through and through, and as the war progressed, he decided that it was up to him to act as an agent of the Confederacy on enemy soil. He established the Knights of the Golden Circle, a secret society that was dedicated both to helping the Southern cause, and to spreading the influence of the slave trade in a "golden circle" across the face of the world.

Although there is much speculation and little in the way of facts concerning this bizarre lodge of shadowy figures, one thing is sure: They engaged in sabotage and criminal activities, using their influence and collective wealth to hamper the cause of the Union as far as they were able. For a time, this subversive society remained secret. However, suspicion soon cast its eye at the noble visage of Dr. Bowles, and he was eventually found out, being sentenced to death.

Not long afterward, Abraham Lincoln stepped forward, and reduced the sentence of Dr. Bowles to life imprisonment, ironically assuring that he would be allowed to return, eventually, to his French Lick home, which he did after the close of the war.

Although he lived a reportedly uneventful life till his death in 1871, he very well may have felt as if his time at French Lick Springs wasn't yet finished, for upon his death, strange events began to transpire around the grand old hotel. By this time, the old hotel was under new management, being the property of enterprising entrepreneur Thomas Taggart, who renovated the building in the wake of massive fire damage, until it became a popular tourist destination for the rich and famous. Presidents, movie stars, and even more infamous personages have nestled themselves well within the confines of those hallowed halls down through the decades.

It soon became apparent, over the years of traffic, that those who left their energy in the wake of their passing through the French Lick Springs Hotel might have accumulated such a fount of energy and thought, dreams and nighttime visions, that it would be little wonder if such a stately old edifice soon acquired the reputation of being haunted. Sure enough, in time, that is exactly what transpired.

The ghost of Tom Taggart, it is said, can be seen as a fleeting phantom, lingering in the doorway of an elevator that seems hell bent on frustrating the capacity for quiet, reasonable logic of anyone who happens to step aboard.

It has been rumored to visit floors not pushed for, the doors swinging open and shut of their own accord, and the heavy scent of old tobacco still curls its snake-like stench through hallways and corridors where smoking hasn't been permitted in years.

Worst of all, the staff of the French Lick Springs Resort all claim to be terrified of working on the sixth floor, as it seems to be a sort of a nucleus or focal point for all the haunting happenings.

Strange shadows and bizarre voices have been known to flit from darkened corners, and accentuate the cold, chill spots and strange atmosphere of menace that permeates this floor. Footsteps abound where no feet are walking, and echoes of a music not heard in many years can be gathered in sundry snatches by the sensitively attuned.

Worst of all, a certain room has become a frequent calling place, much to the perturbation of the desk staff. It seems that, occasionally, calls will originate from the room, even when it is unoccupied by guests. The calls are always silent, and the only sound in the background is the natural ambience of the air-conditioning. Believe it, or not.

Evansville

Of course, ghosts are known to frequent even the most mundane of places. Witness the elusive "Grey Lady" of the Evansville Public Library. Built in 1885, the Willard Library has stood for over a century on the corner of First Avenue as a cultural and intellectual center for Evansville. Easily the oldest building in Indiana, it is listed on the

National Register of Historic Places, and its wealth of records and huge collection of volumes render it a priceless place of learning for those seeking to gather information in the areas of genealogy or Indiana history.

It is also, reputedly, a place a ghost hunter might wish to stop for a visit.

The unearthly ingénue made her debut one lonely night in 1937, when the library janitor, making a routine stop in the library basement found himself confronted with a seeming intruder: A woman dressed in ghastly gray, with a chalk-white face that belied not so much as a fillip of anything easily recognizable as an earthly expression. She apparently vanished as quickly as she had come, and soon was followed by the janitor, who in short order had quit his job and had to be replaced. Soon, even his replacement left, and the library administrators found they had themselves a problem.

The Grey Lady has been reported many times over the long decades since 1937, and even the high, cloying scent of her perfume is reported to be smelled wafting through the tall, grim stacks of the old library. There are numerous (countless, really) reports of desks moving mysteriously about, chairs being pulled across the floor by invisible hands, books flying from shelves, and even a phantom faucet that turned itself on in a locked bathroom.

The most unnerving aspect of the Grey Lady's spectral reign seems to be the several incidents involving her haunting of a longtime librarian—at the woman's home!

Apparently, during the closing and subsequent renovation of the Grey Lady's cherished Children's Reading Room, she commenced to harass the head librarian at her own house, following the woman home in her car, and eventually taking up residence for a short while in her home. There she made a typical appearance, veiled in ghostly gray and redolent in putrid perfume.

During her status as an uninvited guest, she apparently played hell with the lady's nerves, tossing her possessions about, hiding personal items, and rendering certain parts of the home inexplicably cold and drafty.

Of course, it was not long before the Grey Lady found her way home, and again took up residence as the macabre mascot of Willard Library.

Who is she? Well, the theories abound, but one idea has her as the jealous daughter of the man responsible for building the building in the first place. Whether or not this assertion should be taken as gospel truth is strictly up to the judgment of each individual, but the relevant facts are:

Louise Carpenter was the daughter of Willard Carpenter who originally built the building in 1885 as a final present to his beloved hometown. Enraged that her father should so foolishly squander such a huge amount of money, she sought in vain after his death to acquire compensation from the city itself. Withering out her last days in a bitter funk because of her lack of legal recourse, some say she has returned from beyond to take up permanent residence in the building that caused her such consternation during her life.

According to one source, however, a professional psychic was brought in to divine the mystery of the Grey Lady, and yielded the intriguing information that she saw a forlorn woman dressed in ragged grey, staring as if in wonder into a pool of water.

The library was built on land that was, at one point, marshy and covered in water. The recurring vision seemed to suggest a woman that had drowned, possibly in a time too remote for human memory to have ever captured.

Or perhaps this was simply a metaphor, a way of retelling the ancient story of Narcissus, caught forever in a hell of his own making, staring at the beauty and wonder or his eternal reflection. Whatever the objective truth, we can be assured, even as young minds are fostered and nurtured in the halls of Willard Library, there is one walking among them who listens to their murmuring speech as they read the words that dance along dusty pages.

Crown Point

It is getting late, and our time is growing short. It's a pity that all good things must come to end, but that is the eternal cycle of all things. Birth and death—and, some believe, rebirth—follow each other like sunrise and sunset. Our carriage has come to the darkest part of the forest, and is struggling its way through the brambles and muck, while our horses are growing tired of their great burden. So, nestle deeper into the hay and pull your jacket around your shoulders, because we've ridden well past midnight, and everyone knows that it is always darkest before the dawn.

In a strange stretch of land near Crown Point, located off of Interstate 65, just north of Route 2, is the "Gypsy's Cemetery," a forlorn necropolis where once the unjustly persecuted Romany people, while traveling through Indiana in 1820, buried their dead after a harsh winter and a terrible epidemic that ravaged their nomadic community.

It was, of course, no good imploring the bigoted townspeople for any aid and assistance; the prevailing prejudices of the time, coupled with the perceived racial differences, made this a notion that was at best farfetched. If anyone did offer any of the Gypsy travelers aid or comfort during this harsh winter, then certainly the reputed curse that was left upon the land after the Gypsies had finally vacated the following Spring was not intended for them.

The townspeople of Crown Point did everything in their power to wash the lingering presence of the hated Gypsies from their collective minds, but it was in vain. The pitiful collection of makeshift grave markers they left behind for their dead bore testament to the destructive power of human bigotry. The townsfolk must have felt the first flickers of shame, and to try and soothe their shaken conscious eventually converted the burial ground to their own use, interring their own dear departed side by side with the hated Gypsies, mingling their dead, amazingly, with the dead of people they must have considered "pagan" or "devilish."

This did little, however, to deter the legend of the curse over the years, as with the passing of time, the legends of the Gypsy curse upon Crown Point and the Gypsy Cemetery began to reach outlandish proportions.

Purportedly, a Bible carried onto the cursed place may begin to burst into flames. Although you will forgive us for, perhaps, being skeptical at this peculiar notion, you will no doubt be unsurprised to find us highly doubtful about the next nugget of lore. Namely: The idea that those who walk through the ancient burying ground when the spirits are restless are apt to find that the bottoms of their pants are stained red, as if they have been walking through blood.

As if that wasn't enough, the area is notorious for its strange, glowing aerial orbs, which are seen floating over the ground and are rumored to even chase automobiles (and, we may assume, a few unlucky pedestrians) from time to time.

A notable manifestation is the strange "ghost fire" which has been reported to cling close to the ground. It has been reported that vague silhouettes of ghostly figures can be seen dancing around the fire, fighting eternally to keep their bones from freezing in the bitter winter wind, while their more comfortable neighbors rested within their homes, oblivious to the human suffering and death taking place almost within their midst.

Lake County

We are coming to the end now, dear reader, of our ghastly tour through the unsullied pathways of spectral truth. As the fire burns low in so many camps, and the coals sizzle to freezing amid ash-choked hearths, we have time for one more scary saga, a tale of traveling unknown roads that seems only too perfect to wind up our quick tour of the netherworld of ghosts and haunted places.

There is a road that stretches through Lake County, Indiana, called Reeder Road. Its history, sure enough, is a tragic one. We will explain in a moment, but first let us acquaint you with the story of a young man who, having just gotten his license, was enjoying the luxury of driving his automobile in the country one chilly day when, standing upon the shoulder of the road, he happened upon the wan, freezing figure of a young woman, dressed as if she were going to a party.

He pulled over, leaned out, and asked her if she needed a lift, feeling as if it must be his lucky day. The young woman seemed a bit confused, but she looked around as if to see if anyone was watching her, and slid in the passenger side door, shutting it securely behind her.

Immediately, the boy realized there was something odd about the young woman: Her clothing, for instance, was badly dated, almost as if she were planning on attending a costume ball. She looked like she would be comfortable at an old-fashioned sock hop.

He suddenly realized that not only were her teeth chattering, and her hands shaking, but her clothing was wet, as if she had been walking in the rain. He asked her—partly from politeness, partly, we must assume, to protect the upholstery of his car—if she would like to put on his jacket.

"Yes, thank you," she must have replied, and then said, " My name is Elizabeth. I need to get home now. Could you take me?"

She gave him directions, and he replied that it would be no problem whatsoever. As he drove along, he also noted the peculiar chill that had settled over him; suddenly it was freezing in his car, as he sat next to her. He wondered, for a moment, if she wasn't afflicted with some strange disease.

To get to where she wanted to go, they had to drive past Rose Cemetery, and he started to turn to her and make a joke when she asked him, imploringly, if he could pull over to the shoulder of the road. She seemed, all of a sudden, as if she were on the verge of sheer panic.

Not knowing what to make of her bizarre behavior, he did as she asked, and brought the car to a skidding halt in the dusty gutter a few feet away from the cemetery entrance. Before he could say anything, and quite to his surprise, the strange girl flung open the door and leaped from the passenger seat still wearing his jacket. She ran into the old cemetery, and he lost sight of her as she receded into shadow. Perturbed, he stopped the engine and went after her, imploring her to get back in the car, that he would drive her all the way home and that this sort of behavior wasn't necessary.

He had lost her though, and as he went glumly back to the car, he now found himself in a sort of quandary. The girl, whoever she was, was clearly disturbed, but what if she went and told her parents that he had tried to attack or rape her? She had his jacket, and though whoever she lived with must know how mentally ill she was, circumstances taken together might look like something that they were not. He decided that he should drive ahead to the house and see if she was there, and then try to explain things.

By the time he finally found the place, at the top of a weed-choked hill surrounded by overhanging trees, he secretly felt a kind of creeping anxiety gripping the back of his neck. The place looked deserted, as far as he could tell, and the driveway up the hill was a mass of potholes and clumps of weed shooting up through the dirt like spidery fingers made of green. He parked in front of the sagging porch and surveyed the black windows, many of which were thick with dust, broken, and crying out to be boarded over. The whole place looked, strangely, as if it were about to be condemned.

Bracing himself, he knocked at the door, and then listened. Faintly, he heard a scuffling in side, and then knocked a bit louder. Finally, the door swung open a crack, and an older lady (though, admittedly, not anywhere near as old as he had expected) suddenly appeared. She looked like she might be one of his high school teachers.

"May I help you?" the woman asked. She looked as if she were in no mood for nonsense.

The young man stood there for a moment, unsure of how to proceeded, before finally stating:

"Yes, I'm sorry to disturb you Ma'am, but I was given this address by a girl I gave a ride to a few hours ago. She said this was her home. She…she got upset, I guess, and jumped out of the car. She ran into the graveyard. I just thought that I should come out here and see if she was okay."

The woman looked at him for a moment with a stone cold stare, her mouth set rigidly as she looked through him. He began to feel very uncomfortable.

"A young girl? Are you certain, young man?"

"Yes," he said, "She said he name was Elizabeth. And she gave this address."

The woman was silent for a moment.

"Well, all I can tell you is that no one lives here anymore. Not since my mother died last year. I was just out here to look the old place over. You see, I've been thinking of renovating it and turning it into a bed and breakfast."

The young man was, understandably, very confused, and the woman must have sensed this. She suddenly softened her tone somewhat and said, "You know, Mother talked of this occasionally. But I wasn't sure if she was being serious, or if it was just the signs of senility. She claimed that this happened once before, a young man coming to the door, telling her that he had just given a ride to my sister Elizabeth."

The young man, not thinking as quickly as he might have, said, "So a girl named Elizabeth does live here?"

"Did," she said with an air of irritation. "Now, do I look like I am young enough to have a teenage sister?"

"I don't understand."

"Neither do I," she replied, more curtly. "My sister Elizabeth died several decades ago, when she was still a teenager. They found her body lying out in the rain. Hit and run driver; they never found the person responsible. You say she ran into the graveyard, you can go and find her there. I don't think these sorts of pranks are very funny, and the old woman you've been tormenting is gone now. I suggest you get gone, too. Now, if you'll excuse me—"

And with that, she retreated into the gloom of the house, slamming the door securely behind her. He stood there dazed for a moment, and then, with trembling legs, turned and walked back to his car, his head a mass of confusion. He got inside slowly, turned the key, and began to drive.

He ended up, much as he suspected, at the cemetery where last he had seen "Elizabeth" disappear. He wandered, as if in a trance, through the little dips and hills, and through the rows of craggy, weathered tombstones that huddled under forlorn tress, their branches nearly touching the ground like great withered fingers. Finally, he happened upon the thing he had been seeking.

It was his jacket, laid halfway across a headstone. As he bent with trembling fingers to pick it up, he read the name "Elizabeth" carved into the worn surface. Time had started to obliterate the name from the face of the stone, but it was still readable.

He felt his mind begin to crack, and a freezing chill settled over him as he turned and walked quickly away from the cemetery and the headstone of the girl to whom he had given a ride, only hours before.

And now, dear reader, our little tour of the haunted forest beneath the Hoosier moon has come to an end. The horses are weary, and the sun is rising in the east, dispelling the darkness and cold. As you depart for happier places, just remember: It does no good looking over your shoulder for spirits and spooks. They already know where you're at, anyway…

Florence Bly

There is a certain energy one associates with an old
building, particularly any place that has seen eighty
years of comings and goings, tragedies and celebrities,
the famous and the infamous. Such a place is the Hotel
Roberts of Muncie, Indiana. And befitting an hotel of
such a dignified and historic presence, the Hotel Roberts
is, of course, said to be haunted.

The Hotel Roberts has seen many intriguing and
strange characters pass through its doors since business-
man Lou Thornburg first opened his venerable establishment in 1923. Joan Crawford, Bob Hope, and a host
of other celebrities have graced the "Hotel Bob" over
the decades. Famous New York socialite Harriet Mitchell
Bell Anthony, also known as "Diamond Heels" because
of her ostentatious and frequently bizarre fashion sense,
roared the twenties through, partly ensconced within the
weathered stone of the historic hotel.

Of course, less savory personages have also been associ-
ated with the hotel. It was here that infamous outlaw and
murderer Gerald Chapman, known to crime historians by
his unique sobriquet of "The Professor," was apprehended
in Muncie while staying at the Roberts. There is still a downstairs area, right off from the old soda fountain which was
once known as Barney's, where Chapman would sit each
morning at the window, reading his paper and staring off
down the street in case he saw police cars pull up.

Barney's, incidentally, use to boast the comedic styl-
ings of one of the original members of the Keystone Cops.

In short, this hotel has seen a little piece of history move within its walls.

Darker rumors surround the activities of local organized crime during Prohibition. The hotel is said to have been a meeting place for local hoodlums and gangsters, and a place where justice was sometimes "meted out" to those who deserved it. This author, however, has nothing more than hearsay to go on, as far as that particular rumor is concerned.

What is beyond dispute, however, is the presence of a ghostly woman who some say is the spirit of a woman who met a tragic death during Muncie's first "blackout" experiment, following Pearl Harbor.

The woman was anything but a celebrity. She was, in fact, a librarian from a small town several miles away, and it is anyone's guess as to why she was staying at the Hotel Roberts that fateful night. Her family and small circle of acquaintances confirmed that she hadn't been feeling well; she was on a sixty-day leave of absence from her job, supposedly due to "nervous illness." Some have speculated she was having an affair with a married man, or was in love with a hoodlum she was desperately trying to extricate herself from. Whatever the case, Florence Bly would never leave Muncie—or the Hotel Roberts—alive.

We can well imagine her looking out her sixth floor window as lights winked out all over town. Up and down the street, the curtain of absolute darkness fell like a shroud of gloom. It is said she was leaning out of her window wearing her full winter coat, and carrying her purse. It was as if she had been planning on leaving. If so, she could hardly have chosen a more tragic exit.

When the lights were turned back on over the city, the crumpled, bloody figure of a woman lay on the sidewalk below the window from which she had plummeted. A night watchman found her first, and alerted authorities. *The Muncie Star* reported the bizarre details of Florence Bly's unconventional ending. The first thought that the policeman must have entertained was: Was it murder?

Inside her purse was a small card bearing the inscription, "In event of accidental death, please take me to the Meeks Mortuary," an oddly significant clue, considering that Florence Bly was not a local to Muncie. The door to her room was locked from the inside, and the only way a perpetrator could have escaped after throwing Ms. Bly to her death would have been to climb out on the sixth-story ledge and into an adjoining room. Not an impossible feat, but one no halfway-intelligent individual would dare attempt.

It seemed more likely that Florence Bly had simply had enough of the world, and when the lights went down in the small Indiana city of Muncie, she chose that moment to fling herself downward to the supposed sweet balm of death. Why then, the reader must wonder, would she need to be wearing her coat and carrying her purse?

The coroner's office finally ruled the death "accidental."

There will always be unanswered questions as to the true details behind the death of Florence Bly. Of course, the death is only part of the story. There are those who would swear that Florence, while her body has been moldering in the earth since 1943, still nonetheless walks with ghostly steps through the aging corridors of the old hotel. They see her there, a forlorn woman in black, still pining out her agony of a life she couldn't bear.

She is said to appear in the guise of a matronly woman in black clothing, wandering through the hallways or standing in the lobby of the Hotel Roberts, waiting for the clerk to appear and check her in for the very last time.

What's more, she is also said to appear to those standing outside the Roberts, looking up at the row of windows on the sixth floor from across the street.

On moonlit nights she is said to appear in the window from which she fell to her death. Always, she is a faceless person in somber black, bereaved unto eternity.

I can vouchsafe for the fact that the ghost of Florence Bly exists. I have seen her with my own eyes.

The first time I explored the Hotel Roberts was with a group of friends studying psychic phenomenon. I knew nothing, at the time, of any supposed haunting that took place there. Yet upon entering I was struck, suddenly, at how life imitated art: The Hotel Roberts will, immediately, remind those who are literate, or in with pop culture, of the Overlook Hotel, the fictional haunted house in Stanley Kubrik's movie adaptation of Stephen King's classic horror novel, *The Shining*. Even with substantial remodeling, the palpable sense of age—of spent energy, of people thinking lonely thoughts in the wee hours of the morning—hits you immediately, and becomes stifling after spending many hours walking through the hallways. After a while, the maze-like halls and the bizarre sense of timelessness seem to put you into a sort of creeping trance, and you really feel as if, in some sense, a building can operate as a time machine or gateway device to receive flickers of imagery and sound that have long since passed away.

Going up to the first floor mezzanine, I was struck by the old pictures adorning the walls. Each of them, in their own peculiar way, were tangible ghosts: Images from an era, a moment of time that was no more, yet was captured forevermore in that one brief flashbulb—a shot of a reality none now living can ever know. I also discovered, not surprisingly, that there were "hidden" images in some of them.

In one of the photos, the enigmatic image of a woman's face seems to appear in the chance glare upon a highly-polished floor. In still another, a more disturbing example is a picture of an old jazz band set up in one of the ballrooms in front of a set of glass doors, seeming normal enough at first. However, upon closer inspection, one can see the faint image of a ghostly woman staring out from behind the glass. Some would say this is a chance reflection of the singer, but the image seems to, clearly, be that of a female. Who was she? Why does she seem to be nearly a mirage?

Walking the corridors, one can feel the energy, in the dead of night, begin to stir. It is the energy of age, of tired feet and twirling thoughts cast out into the vapors; it is the spent energy of tears that the psychically sensitive can tune into, and that most everyone more sensitive than a stone mallet can feel—to some degree.

The rooms we walked past that night all bore the names of famous dead celebrities: there was a "Clark Gable Suite," a " Scarlet O'Hara Suite," a "Bob Hope Suite," and even a "John Dillinger Suite." These names all hearken back to the early years of the twentieth century and a simpler, some would say more elegant, day and age.

My own first trip to the Hotel Roberts yielded no small amount of paranormal phenomena: Cold spots, intense feelings of oppression and suffocating pressure, and of all things, what I take now to be the ghost of Florence Bly.

Before I explain, I should take a moment to first address the bizarre stench that appeared for a brief moment on one of the floors, in an open area off the back elevators. It could only be smelled by myself and one other person present. Our other companions never smelled a thing. I could feel the icy prickles of realization that told me the stench was the unearthly fetor of death. Perhaps it was a whiff of odor from the other side.

Later, while walking through the halls as a group, we could feel the pressure of something standing in front of us, hidden partly in shadow, as we pushed against a growing heat. At one point, I realized that we were surrounded by spirit, and that, for some reason, tonight was a particularly active night, in an occult sense.

Finally, as we were preparing to leave, we went down to the first floor mezzanine to take one final walkabout before calling it a night. I was sauntering slowly across the carpet, looking out over the railing into the lobby below, when suddenly I saw what appeared to be a drab, black-clad woman standing at the desk below as if about to check in. I stopped for a moment, rubbing my eyes and wondering if I was imagining things, when I realized that she was standing perfectly still. Then, as if she was nothing more than an image in a movie, she seemed to fade into the shadows of the background, and was gone.

My guides later took me across the street and told me to look up at the windows of the sixth floor. Lo and behold, I did so, and saw what appeared to be a woman standing at the window, looking out into the street below.

At the time, I had no idea who Florence Bly was, nor did I know her story, or that the hotel was reputed to be haunted at all. Later, having gone to the Special Collections room at Bracken Library on the Ball State campus, I was privileged to find a small booklet that detailed the entire story, and explained the appearance of the ghost as well.

Things began to make sense for awhile. And then, they did not.——

Our Haunted State?

One of the strangest stories I know of happened in South Bend, Indiana in the early part of the last century.

The citizens of South Bend pride themselves on their level-headedness and their old fashioned family values, and given this, they have very little time for any foolishness. So, when the words "Remember Pearl Harbor!" appeared one day chalked on a cement car park, no one paid it very much attention, although they did remember the enigmatic phrase.

Unfortunately, it meant little to them at the time, for the Japanese attack on Pearl Harbor was still two years in the future!

Do ghosts travel through time? No one can ever know the answer to this, I'm afraid, but one thing is for certain: The above anecdote was one of many such baffling stories preserved in the weird writings of Indiana radio host Frank Edwards. Edwards was a Hoosier treasure, a sort of Midwestern Ripley (of *Ripley's Believe it or Not*) who compiled in books—such as *Strange People* and *Stranger Than Science*—a catalogue of astounding oddities. Everything from mysterious creatures, to ghosts and the psychic wolf was grist for the mill where Edwards was concerned. Before he died tragically of a heart condition, he had written what was probably the first set of books by a Hoosier on the then relatively new phenomenon of UFOs: *Flying Saucers—Serious Business*, and *Flying Saucers—Here and Now*. It was shortly after the publication of these two books that he laid down on the couch one evening, complaining to his wife of not feeling well, and died suddenly.

Frank Edwards was truly one of Indiana's own historical treasures. Another, less well known son of the Hoosier state was the inimitable Harold Sherman, who once spent a year writing for the newspaper—*The Chronicle Tribune*—of my own hometown of Marion, before setting off to Hollywood to write screenplays, such as the one he wrote for the classic film *The Adventures of Mark Twain.*

Although Sherman began his career as a sports writer, he left this world as an enthusiastic believer in the supernatural and author of many books on spiritualism, ghosts, psychic powers, and the life hereafter. His turn of mind happened, interestingly enough, while he was working for the *Chronicle* in Marion, at the old Marion Hotel.

Sherman had been sent by his paper to cover a lecture by Chicago police officer Harry Loose, who was currently making the rounds of the Chataqua Red Path lecture circuit, giving talks about the evils of gangs and the necessity of temperance. Sherman waited until after the lecture to approach Loose, and the two men discovered, immediately, they had a friendly affinity. Sherman mentioned that he was, although skeptical, passably interested in psychic phenomena. Loose responded that he himself was a psychic and that if Sherman wanted to be made a believer, he should accompany him back to his hotel room for a demonstration.

As Sherman would confess later, Loose performed "psychic miracles" in front of him that evening at the old Marion Hotel, demonstrating levitation, telepathy, and clairvoyance. Skeptical people will claim that this was nothing more than clever parlor tricks, but whatever the case, they turned Harold Sherman from a skeptic to a believer that night.

It would take years, but eventually Loose would convince Sherman and his wife to join him in Chicago, where a group of like-minded individuals had taken it upon themselves to organize and edit a massive work of channeled messages, received from "Higher Source" entities by the nephew of the famous Dr. John Harvey Kellogg of Battlecreek Sanitarium fame. This text would, eventually, come to be known as the *Urantia Book*, and it is still read today by thousands who seek spiritual inspiration and enlightenment.

Sherman would spend the rest of his life exploring the world of the psychic and supernatural, and upon his death was personally convinced that his soul would survive in some form in a world beyond.

We discuss this information, primarily, to establish the pedigree of Indiana as a place where the world of the supernatural and the world of the mundane have frequently met and crossed into one another. There are as many coincidences, strange happenings, and historical personages springing from here as you'll find anywhere.

Both Sherman and Edwards, as men given to intense interest in the supernatural, undoubtedly visited historic Camp Chesterfield at least once during their lives. Located in the small town of Chesterfield, just minutes away from Muncie, Camp Chesterfield was founded by Spiritualist John Westerfield in the late 1800s. Several of the houses sitting on the grounds were once used as stops on the Underground Railroad, Spiritualists being the strongest proponents of Abolitionism. Of course, their more orthodox Christian brethren saw fit to slander and disparage them in any way possible, thus leading to accusations of fraud and phony mediumship.

To be fair, there are some workers on the spectral path who have resorted to cheap tricks when their powers were waning; there have also been outright charlatans who used many time-tested magic tricks to fake ghostly phenomena at Spiritualist séances: Having confederates slip around the darkened room, dressed in glowing chiffon, or using slight of hand to produce objects and then claiming spirits left them in their wake. This is old hat to fraudulent mediums, as well as table-tipping, phony slate writing, and phony levitation tricks.

However, just because some unscrupulous persons have resorted to trickery in the past is no reason to be dismissive of spiritualism, which must today stand as the foremost religion dedicated to breaking through the barrier that separates the world of matter and spirit. The Spiritualists of today seek to find that nucleus of truth that rests at the heart of every major religion. To be truthful, this author can't say that they are far off the mark.

The historic grounds of Camp Chesterfield roll pleasantly into a little dip between hills, marked by a gorgeous old fountain, and by monuments that harken back to the idea that all religions are one and spirit is eternal. There is a representational monument of a Native American, a stone pyramid, various statuettes of saints, and a sort of stone crescent with a semicircle of busts of various world religious figures. Buddha, Mohammed, and Lao Tze sit side by side with Zeus and Confucious. At the head of this assemblage is a bust of Jesus Christ. Various benches seem to encourage the weary to sit in contemplative harmony with these august personages.

There is also a bizarre sort of stone grotto, the "Garden of Prayer," which can be entered and is presided over by a statue of Christ. During the annual psychic fair, one can enter the little stone building, read the quotes from famous mediums marked in stone on the wall, and leave a candle of a saint burning in quiet testament to prayer. I usually leave an offering of small coins, or one of my books.

Lest you think that Camp Chesterfield is run-down or outdated, think again: It boasts a modern cafeteria, a bookstore, a cathedral where classes on mediumship and psychic powers are held, and an assortment of well-kept houses, many of which advertise—on a little sign in the front yard—the services and specialties offered by the particular medium within. This is truly a neighborhood out of an offbeat film.

On my first visit to a Spiritualist church service (held in a little chapel on the grounds), I was surprised at how much like a regular Christian service the worship was, up until the point a resident medium stepped forward and began to call forward information from various spirits connected with the parishioners. I myself was given information from a deceased relative that the medium had no way of knowing, since I had never before set foot inside the building or met anyone remotely connected with the camp.

At one point, she began to draw impressions of various individual's "spirit guides," passing them to people in the audience. I was fairly impressed.

There is also a hotel there, the Sunflower, but I have no idea if it is haunted or not. I would guess it probably is, but there are so many spirits roaming the ground at Camp Chesterfield, who could possibly be bothered by one or two solitary hotel haunts?

Case in point: I am usually a vendor at the annual Camp Chesterfield "Spirit Fest," and I have a booth where I sell a variety of my books and videos (many from my personal collection). During the event, which is several hours long during the morning and afternoon of September 17, I also try to find a little bit of that special spirit myself; try to recharge my psychic batteries, so to speak. So, leaving a friend at my booth, I trudged down the little footpath that leads to the stone grotto, the "Garden of Prayer."

The stone gate was open, and as I went inside, I saw the Catholic saint candles that worshippers had left in my wake. I quickly thrust a hand in my pocket and put down a few coins as an offering.

It was not the first time I had been in the Garden of Prayer: I had actually visited it once before and sat down on the little stone bench, looking up at the statue of Christ in reverie. My mother soon walked in, and she said immediately that she felt as if she had been here before, as if she meant in another life.

My mother certainly doesn't believe in reincarnation. Later, after standing there a few minutes, we both agreed on one thing: A palpable sense of heavy, vibrating energy permeated the Garden of Memory. It was a sort of electric pulse, very strong, and also a little frightening.

During this visit, I walked through the archway to my right, into another, smaller room, with a stained-glass window depicting the Star of David. It lent an eerie glow to this adjoining room. Here, as in the front room, was a statue of Christ, similar to the one out front, but more primitive. The room itself had an air of even greater holiness because it was separate, smaller, and darker than the front chamber.

At the foot of this Christ were the same familiar candles, and I quickly left a few coins here as well. I then sat down on the little iron bench in front, and started to concentrate. Suddenly, in the flickering light from fading candles, I saw something that happened so fast it astounded me. At first, I didn't even realize what had transpired.

For a split second, I had seen tears of blood roll from the eyes of that statue and vanish. Call it imagination if you will, but I did see it.

I left the garden of Memory that day with a greater appreciation for the spirits of Camp Chesterfield than ever before, and a greater understanding of our haunted state.

Mr. Death Comes Calling

My next tale for you came to me first as a bit of apocrypha: I can't vouchsafe for the veracity of this particular gem, but I can say that when it first was told to me around a campfire one evening while camping out in high school, it seemed to me to smack of the truth, and even seemed strangely familiar. It takes place during that most spectral of all seasons, Christmas, a ghostly time when the ancient story of Scrooge again takes prominence on late-night cable television.

This story takes place in Marion during the Depression, and it involves a typical family struggling to make ends meet. If we try for a moment, we can step back through the doorway of our mind's eye, and journey through the years to the front yard of this little home. Looking in the window, we can see the mother as she hurriedly tries to prepare an all too meager Christmas dinner.

The father has just gotten up and put on his coat. With shovel in hand, he heads for the back kitchen door, walking past his wife as if nothing is wrong. She hurriedly gets up from putting a pot in the oven and says, "Bill, you're not going out on Christmas Day, are you?"

The husband, who had every intention of staying in bed, reminds her that times are tough, and they could use the extra money he can make shoveling out walkways. Somewhere, Junior and his brother have stirred, and one might be sitting on the stairs, reading a battered old comic.

She leans forward, kisses him, and says, "I am the luckiest woman in the world. Just be back soon, and be safe. Okay?"

He promises her that he will, and in the meantime, she hurries to prepare dinner. After an hour or so, the smell coming from the kitchen is sumptuous, and both boys start to sneak peeks into the broiling pot before their mother shoos them away. Upstairs still is a little sister, the baby of the family, very ill with what the doctor thinks might be pneumonia.

It is another hour before the boys help their mother set the table, and the family sits down, still waiting for the father to appear. Later, the mother will take a bowl of chicken broth upstairs and try to get her daughter to eat. For now, though, she is starving, and she glances up out the kitchen window as she fiddles with pots and pans, expecting her husband to come sauntering through the snow covered backyard, up the walk, and through the backdoor with his boots covered in snow. She waits, starting to get anxious, and finally she sees his familiar, comforting shape emerge starkly against the grey and white world outside. Strangely, though, he is accompanied by another man.

She goes to the back door and looks outside. Most definitely, he is walking side-by-side with a man who looks like he might be some old hobo, or bindle-stiff.

"Bill!" she calls out. "Dinner is ready."

He smiles at her, and then says: "This is a friend of mine. I invited him in for dinner. He's all alone this year, you see."

She looks at him, a little perturbed, but says nothing and invites the strange man into their home to sit at their table. He is very quiet, and dressed in a black fedora, black coat, black trousers, and patched boots that look a size too large for him. She sums him up, in her mind, as a hobo, but he looks even stranger than that. Like a ragged old undertaker.

Her sons look at each other apprehensively, so she quiets their doubts by saying, "Boys, your father has invited a guest over for Christmas dinner today. This is Mister…sorry, I didn't get your name."

"You can call me Mr. Sheaves," he says slowly; his voice has a strange hollow ring to it.

"Yes, well, pleasure to meet you Mr. Sheaves. Boys, isn't it a pleasure to have Mr. Sheaves with us this afternoon?"

Neither of them say anything, and the family begins to eat, when they become all too frightfully aware that their father and the strange man aren't touching their food. The wife says, "Well, boys, dig in," but the men continue to sit staring, albeit with strangely serene looks on their faces.

She leans over to see if she can smell alcohol on her husband, but notices none. She says, "Look, I worked damn hard to give you this meal today. The least you can do is bother to eat it. I know you must be starving."

The two men continue to sit there, silently, and suddenly, the wife becomes upset. She rises, picks up a bowl, goes to the counter and grabs a ladle, and begins to spoon broth into the bowl, all the while saying: "I don't know what type of game you boys are playing, whether you've had a snoot full or not, but I never thought I'd live to see the day my husband would act like a total moron in front of his family. Now, I'm going to go upstairs and feed our daughter, Bill, and when I come down, maybe you'll have snapped out of it."

Frightened, she takes the bowl upstairs, leaving her two boys downstairs, munching apprehensively, with her husband and the bizarre Mr. Sheaves. She goes down the little hall and into her daughter's room,

The child is lying in a little bundle beneath her blankets, and she sets the soup down on the dresser, nudging her gently to try and rouse her from her sleep. Then she notices the child's face rapidly turning blue, and she hears the small, suffocating sound of her trying to get her breath. Something is desperately wrong. She yells for her family, and the eldest son comes charging up the stairs. She turns and tells him to run next door and call an ambulance.

She goes to the top of the stairs and calls her husband, then hurries down, only to find her small boy still sitting at the table with tears in his eyes. She has no time to concern herself with him, however. She leans out the back door, yelling at her son to hurry, and then charges back upstairs. The child is, apparently, still alive, although she looks like she is on the edge of death.

It is an agonizing few minutes before the ambulance arrives, and the child is rushed to the hospital, where by a thin margin she survives her bout with pneumonia and her close brush with death. The mother accompanies the ambulance to the hospital, momentarily forgetting everything except the welfare of her gravely ill child.

It was only later, fuming with anger, that she returned home to find her two sons still alone. She thinks that her husband had at last taken leave of his senses and left his family for good. She begins to cry, bitterly, emotionally shattered from the strange events of Christmas Day.

Her sons do not know how to react. Suddenly, there is a knock at the door, and the eldest son goes to answer it. It is a portly man who lives down the road; she knows him from church. He's a policeman.

It is evening now, and has only been a few hours since her daughter was rushed to the hospital and her husband disappeared. The man has a heavy, somber look on his face, and says, "M'am, I'm sorry to have to tell you this, but your husband met with an accident this morning on his way out to shovel snow. He slipped and hit his head on something, and must have laid out in the snow unconscious for hours. We think it was hypothermia that got him."

The realization washes over her in an awesome wave, and she begins to cry more loudly, pressing her hand to her mouth. She stumbles into a chair as the man makes a quiet exit. She is emotionally overwhelmed now, to the point of, perhaps, nervous breakdown. Suddenly, her young son approaches her, and putting and arm around her says: "Ma, don't worry about it. Before Daddy and the man vanished, Daddy told me that he would never be back again, but that he made a deal with Mr. Sheaves so Sissy could stay. Now, heaven will just have to wait for all the rest of us."

2910 North Delaware Street

The idea of the poltergeist, or "noisy ghost," (taken from the German term that traditionally encapsulates haunting phenomena that occurs with a young child as their focus) is one that has riveted Hollywood since American moviegoers first settled down in their theatre seats to watch the exploits of the all-American family so tormented in Stephen Spielberg's special effects blockbuster Poltergeist, which was first released to massive acclaim in the 1980s.

That the phenomenon of poltergeists and what they do to those with the misfortune to become the focal point of their bizarre manifestations is entirely based on the factual experiences of typical, run-of-the-mill folks is beyond dispute: Their recorded activities encompass everything from the sordid saga of the "Bell Witch," to the bottle cap and cork-popping antics that took place in the home of the Herrman family of Long Island, New York during the middle Sixties.

Indianapolis has its own unhallowed history of hysterical haunts when it comes to the subject of poltergeists, and it was at the home of one Mrs. Renate Beck, a woman living with her daughter and elderly mother in a two-story house, where the dreaded noisy ghosts decided to rear their enigmatic heads to frighten and confound the living that dwelled therein.

It was on a March night in 1962 when the first inexplicable incident occurred. Mrs. Beck and her small family had experienced nothing of much concern for the entire day, but had their hands full come nightfall, when a heavy glass beer stein managed to move on its own accord, sailing through the air in a gentle and guided manner, and coming to rest behind a flower-pot. As if this wasn't sufficiently puzzling to catch the attention of the occupants of the house, it was not long afterward that a number of highly strange occurrences began to make themselves known, in a typically cryptic supernatural fashion.

Very soon there was a titanic crash from upstairs, and the three women raced to the source of the noise, fearing that an intruder must have happened upon the premises. Much to their intellectual consternation, the source of the crash proved not to be a would-be burglar, but instead was the shattered remnants of a crystal glass that seemed to have literally taken wings and flown, to its own destruction, toward a shattering impact with the floor.

This, however, was only the beginning.

It was not long before more crystal and glass was shattering, and the family was forced, through dint of sheer nervous exhaustion, to flee the premises and to check into a local hotel. One can only wonder how they must have felt, but they must have known that the odd occurrences, or whatever was behind them, must be just beginning to exert their influence. It was no time before the family found themselves literally besieged by a bizarre panoply of uncomfortable oddities with nothing in the way of explaining their reason or source.

Returning home the next day, the women hoped and prayed that the initial night of freak occurrences was somehow over. They were, however, soon to find themselves disappointed, as glass objects began to shatter around the house again in an alarming manner, and a full, hot cup of coffee sailed through the air, apparently targeting Mrs. Gemmecke, Mrs. Beck's mother, with the scalding contents. The cup shattered harmlessly against a wall, but Mrs. Gemmecke soon felt her nerves give way.

The family soon decided it was time to seek legal intervention, although the curious reader must surely be wondering what on earth good they could have thought it would do. The officer, Ray Patton, confessed himself to be as equally baffled as the tormented home owners, but insisted their must be a logical explanation along the lines of prank pellet shooters or the influence of a hi-fi stereo system somewhere in the vicinity. Needless to say, his theories went largely unappreciated.

By this time, the officer had witnessed the disintegration of a crystal swan by unseen hands, and had been so impressed by the sight that he immediately radioed for backup. The police, going under the "sound terrorism" theory, brought with them special sensitive equipment to apprehend the supposed errant frequencies. Finding that, indeed, the manifestations had nothing to do with sound or radio waves of any kind, they confessed themselves stumped once again, but at least appreciated the fact that their presence had alerted a cavalcade of neighbors to come and watch the bizarre goings-on from across the street. The home was becoming something of a neighborhood wonder, and, eventually, even the newspapers would get in on the act for a little while.

One of the most mysterious of happenings during the entire affair was the situation involving Mrs. Beck's missing purse, which contained 125 dollars cash, and which vanished, quite mysteriously, over the course of the events. Although it must be first accorded that poltergeists, whatever other parameters they may comprise, would seem to have little use for conventional money, a short time later, the purse suddenly reappeared at the feet of Mrs. Gemmecke with all intact save around eighty dollars missing. Mysterious.

The case took a far more frightening and repulsive turn with the appearance of bizarre "puncture" or bite marks on the skin of the women, particularly the youngest daughter. These bizarre wounds are often reported in cases involving malicious spirits, and as in the other cases, these particular wounds seemed to appear instantly, caused no pain, no bleeding, and confounded all rational attempts at categorization.

One set of wounds , on Mrs. Gemmecke's throat, was accompanied by a feeling that she was being "choked." The wounds then seemed to appear on her neck, and eventually turned into bruises. Mysteriously, they did not even sting.

For sixteen terrifying days objects were broken in the Beck house, but the police , having been called in again, amazingly arrested Mrs. Gemmecke! Apparently, the woman was seen by the police throwing objects around during their investigation, and she was thus arrested and charged with making a false report. It took the assurances of Mrs. Beck to convince them that her mother, a diabetic, had been having an nervous attack, and was thus unable to control herself. There were, of course, further strange incidents that Mrs. Gemmecke could not possibly have been responsible for.

One of these involves the private investigations of Indianapolis businessman and Beck family friend Emil Noseda, who was a stalwart companion and investigator during the strange period of poltergeist phenomena. Mr. Noseda catalogued a veritable cornucopia of destructive happenings, from the ripping of feathers from pillows to the moving about of furniture independent of any living agency. Mr. Noseda quickly became a believer of the strange happenings, and confessed himself at a loss as to what in the world could be behind them.

One anecdote involves the family and Mr. Noseda and his wife sitting around the kitchen table in the dark (having a séance?) , when suddenly, alerted by some disturbing noises in the kitchen, they rushed into the dining room to see what was the matter, and were greeted with a startling sight: Several kitchen knives had apparently become dislodged from the rack upon which they were kept, and had rearranged themselves on the floor in the image of a cross. They were soon replaced, and the assembled party left the room, only to have the same occurrence happen again. It was unsettling stuff.

The vast majority of the damage done during the strange, supernatural spell was to furnishings and bric-a-brac, and of course to the nerves of the small family of mother, grandmother, and child. But what could have caused such a bizarre series of occurrences to transpire in the first place?

Opinions vary, but it has been pointed out that Mrs. Beck was recently divorced, and that the divorce had been particularly distressing on the daughter, Linda. Poltergeists do seem to congregate around emotionally disturbed youngsters, and there is some conjecture as to whether or not they constitute actual "hauntings" in the traditional sense, or whether they might simply be a buried manifestation of psychokinetic energy, blowing out like a storm from the subconscious faculty of a young child and erupting across the landscape of their home in destructive fury.

Whatever the case may be, the phenomena grew to include the familiar series of strange "rappings" that accompany so many cases of poltergeist activity, and these were heard upstairs while everyone else was downstairs. Mrs. Gemmecke, as before, soon became a possible suspect, but when the rappings continued even while her hands were being held down by Mr. Noseda, it became clear that some other, unknown faculty was at work.

If anyone reading this should doubt the veracity of the claims made in the preceding, they should consider that no less an authority than the esteemed paranormal investigator William Roll put in an appearance to investigate the claims firsthand. In no short amount of time, he had cataloged over one hundred instances of mysterious movings and willful destruction by invisible agents, as well as over a dozen mysterious wounds appearing on the flesh of Mrs. Beck, Mrs. Gemmecke, and young Linda. In his 1972 book, The Poltetgeist, he featured the case as one that was beyond the reach of the skeptics, and beyond reproach.

Eventually, the luckless family was left alone, the short-lived spurt of newspaper coverage died, and the poltergeist receded back into the murky fabric of the unknown.

Hannah House

Imagine, if you will, a time when being born black in the American South meant being born to a life of cruel slavery, the only escape via the system of the Underground Railroad that led through Northern states, where fleeing slaves might hope to finally attain their freedom.

One such stop of the Underground Railroad was a red brick mansion built in 1858 in Indianapolis, Indiana, and commonly referred to as "Hannah House," after the owner of the home, a state legislator and sheriff named Alexander M. Hannah. A committed Abolitionist, Mr. Hannah used the basement of his home as a hiding place for runaway slaves, securing the liberation of many, and gaining for himself a reputation as a man who lived and died by his Christian conscience.

In the turbulent days leading up to the Civil War, protecting runaway slaves was a risky affair, and, tellingly, a tragic incident did befall the illicit operation, leading those who visit Hannah House today to speculate on whether or not this might have anything to do with the long history of ghostly phenomenon that seems to swirl about the place.

How it happened was a matter of conjecture, but, in some manner, a lantern was carelessly tipped over in the basement, and the resulting fire cost the lives of a number of the luckless slaves who had escaped chains and persecution, only to find themselves robbed of a better life by a cruel trick of fate. Many deaths resulted from the blaze, and the bodies, because they could not be buried properly in a Christian churchyard, were consigned to cheap caskets in the charred basement in which they succumbed, until they could be moved to undisclosed locations and disposed of.

They were not, to be mild, very easy times in which to live and die.

If this were the only tragedy to ever befall the red brick home, it would be enough, but there were further heartaches in store for the Hannah family, as the young wife soon found herself to be pregnant. Elated, the anxious couple eagerly awaited the birth. Unfortunately for them, the cherished infant carried its coffin with it into the world, and the young Mrs. Hannah found herself very ill with the burden of pregnancy. Notably, life went on for Alexander and Elizabeth Hannah, though they remained childless until their deaths.

It was many years later that an Indianapolis psychic, investigating the weird goings-on at Hannah House, insisted that she felt the presence of a stillborn child, an unknown child, haunting an upstairs bedroom. She described accurately the forced birth of a monstrous fetus, and the diseased condition of the mother, who must have been Elizabeth Hannah herself.

This revelation confounded historians, who had no record of a second child being born in an upstairs bedroom, and who insisted that the records showed the birth and death of only one Hannah infant, and that in another part of the house.

It was not until the Hannah family plot was located, along with a tiny stone bearing only the year of death, that it seemed that, incredibly, the vision of the psychic was fully corroborated.

As the years passed, the house changed hands, eventually ending up in the possession of a young man who was left as caretaker by his mother. It was during his attempt at renovation that the strange series of ghostly visitations first painted the old structure with an out of the ordinary brush. As the young man busily went about restoring the dilapidated home one dark, cloudy day, he was alerted immediately to what sounded like a fall of breaking glass in the old basement.

Running to find the source of the disturbance, he was equally mystified to find the basement empty, with no sign that any glass had been broken or that anything else was amiss. As strange as this occurrence was, and as puzzling as the grip of fear that seemed to clutch the young man's heart, there was another strange aspect that began to creep into the manifestations in the following days. This was the unmistakable reek of putrefying flesh that seemed to waft from an upstairs room, and soon filled the house at odd intervals. This was the most overtly unpleasant occurrence, but it was far from the only one.

Strange knocks and bizarre footsteps seemed to echo out of the house at odd hours, and doors firmly shut would swing open of their own accord. The young man, who had inherited the home from his mother, a descendant of the original Hannah family, knew the history of the house well enough to begin to suspect that there were lost souls still wandering the empty halls of Hannah House, crying out in their anguished afterlife for understanding and recognition.

The house changed hands again in 1972, and became the sight of an antique store. The owners also occupied the house for a short time, before deciding that it would be wise to seek more reassuring lodgings. One reason for this might have been the new, bizarre evolution of the resident haunting.

It was one typical business day when the wife of the proprietor, who was manning the store while her husband was away, heard what seemed to be footsteps coming from the closed, upstairs area.

Looking up at the second floor landing, she saw what appeared to be the image of a man dressed in somber black clothing, standing and staring down at her. Frightened, she started up the stairs, calling the strange visitor but receiving no response.

She was amazed when the image of the man, who was dressed in old-fashioned Victorian clothing and mutton-chops, simply seemed to fade before her very eyes.

In time, the house changed hands once again, and it became, over the years, because of its sinister reputation, a sort of local attraction for individuals that find it edifying to be scared out of their wits. When the Jaycees used Hannah House as the setting for their annual "Halloween Spook House" in 1980, the house was refurbished, fitted with spectacular special effects, and proved to be very popular with young children

Of course, not all of the spooky effects were planned fakes. Some of the most mysterious and startling effects happened of their own accord, driven on by an unseen hand.

One story recounted is that of several workers who were taking their lunch break in the old kitchen of Hannah House, when, suddenly, one of them became alerted by the strange, high-pitched sound of scratching coming, seemingly, from nowhere. Though they tried, unsuccessfully, to locate the sound, several hours elapsed and they were no wiser to its origin than before they began.

But that was not all. Hannah House continued to brood, to bear its dark secrets, and to stand like a sentinel against the tide of time. Those that have ventured within have often found themselves at the center of the most puzzling happenings.

The coordinator of the haunted house project, a Mr. Raasch, installed a stereo system to broadcast eerie music and sounds throughout the building while tours were being given. To his amazement one night, while he was sitting with an business associate, the stereo was suddenly switched off. Getting up to see whatever could have happened, he went to examine the controls, and to his amazement, found that the button had been depressed, just as if an invisible someone in the room decided it was high time for a little peace and quiet. Mr. Raasch, nonplussed, pushed the button down and restarted the music, walking back out to join his friend. Amazingly, the machine again shut itself off, and the music stopped, leaving Mr. Raasch to wonder, exactly, how the device could manage to operate itself.

The most interesting happening at Hannah House in recent years was the impromptu tour taken by a news crew who decided to celebrate Halloween one year by filming a special on the premises. As soon as the crew and cameraman entered, one man opined, "Wouldn't it be funny if that chandelier started swinging by itself?"

No sooner had he spoke than, suddenly, it began to move, pendulum-like, back and forth, casting eerie shadows about and startling the onlookers.

Of course, there was not even the hint of a breeze or draft, or anything else to explain why the chandelier should begin to move on its own. But the best was yet to come.

While wrapping up their broadcast, an admittedly nervous news man finished closing his report, when suddenly he was startled from behind by the crash of an immensely old picture to the floor of the old bedroom where they were working. Upon close examination, the reporters were startled to find that the nail upon which the picture rested was still perfectly fitted into the wall, and that the wire holding the picture up was still intact.

They postulated that it would be impossible for the picture to have fallen of its own accord. It would have had to have been lifted up, forward, and allowed to drop from its place.

Lifted by what or whom is a fact they never ascertained.

Old Jacob

One of Indiana's strangest supernatural tales has to do with the story of one local eccentric from Martin County who was well-known as an aged and peculiar old man.

Jacob Cox operated a farm, and was accepted in his small, rural community as quite a character. Jacob was the sort of individual that everyone had a nodding acquaintance with, most had spoken to, and yet few people really seemed to actually know.

It was one strange spring day when a man named Martin Winding , who had journeyed a short way south, came calling on his old friend Jacob Cox, expecting to see the solitary farmer at work, singing to himself, as he was wont to do, while he cared for his livestock.

Mr. Winding, not being familiar with the latest goings-on in the community, rode his horse up to the old house, and suddenly found himself perplexed to note that the place seemed strangely vacant. A quick perusal on horseback seemed to confirm to him that something had changed very drastically since his short time away, and he rode up to the barn, getting off his steed only long enough to investigate for himself, and ascertain that, indeed, the animals were gone, the house was vacant, and the farm (judging from the overgrown yard and unkempt fields) seemed to have been completely abandoned.

He got up on his horse, wondering what in the world must be going on, and began to ride away when suddenly, looking over his shoulder, saw, to his amazement, old Jacob Cox emerge from the darkened barn, and begin to walk, quickly past him, as if he were in a trance. The old man began to walk onward, disappearing behind a corn silo, and Mr. Winding called his name, to no avail.

He decided that the old man must not have heard him, and proceeded to urge his horse forward when, amazingly, a strange gust of wind seemed to come up from behind him, taking him by surprise, and to his horror, it was followed by the unmistakable presence of hands grasping his shoulders.

He started forward in panic, not even daring to look behind him at the stranger that had jumped on the back of his horse, and taken him hostage apparently, and galloped quickly forward in sheer terror. By this time, he had forgotten all about Old Jacob, and instead, wondered if he was not being hi-jacked by an outlaw or insane person.

He went down the road, kicking up dust, and finally came to the edge of the Cox property, when he felt the grip around his neck loosen and disappear. Looking about him now, wildly, he saw that there was, in fact, no one sitting on the horse behind him, and the long road in back of him was completely empty. There was no place for any assailant to run and hide, either; the road was surrounded by flat fields on both sides, stretching out to the horizon.

Visibly shaken, the man rode on into town , and settled down at a tavern to talk over his strange experience with a local. The man, at first, seemed not to believe him, until he mentioned that the farm he had just come from was the farm of old Jacob Cox.

The man looked suddenly frightened, and then smiled, asking, "You must be pulling my leg, fellow. You say that you saw Jacob Cox come out of his barn and walk across the yard right in front of you?"

"Yes," answered Mr. Winding. "What of it?"

"Well, I find that pretty hard to believe, Mister, seeing as how Jacob Cox has been dead for over a week now. I guess that must explain the phantom rider that jumped on the back of your horse with you!"

The man took a swallow of beer, laughed, smiled, and must have dismissed whatever doubts and questions that were flitting through his mind beneath a haze of alcohol.

As for Mr. Martin Winding, he was not seen in Martin County ever again.

Stiffy Green

Highland Lawn Cemetery in Terre Haute is the resting place of a canine cadaver that refuses, apparently, to wait out the decades till Judgment quietly. For it is the bark of a small, stiff-legged bulldog, and the strange story of his deathless attachment to his elderly master, that provides us with our next spine-tingling saga.

John Heinl was the master of a small bull terrier with a strange, straight-legged walk and piercing green eyes that was known, locally, as "Stiffy Green." Stiffy was a faithful and obedient pup for many years, and the two were nearly inseparable during the strange, solitary walks that Heinl often took at sunset, when the mystic play of light and shadow seemed to beckon to the poetic nature of some individuals.

For many years, Stiffy Green was a four-legged fixture of the community, a furry friend to children of all ages, and the closest companion that John Heinl could be surmised to have. Many residents fondly remembered, in later years, the walking duo sitting on the old man's porch together, surrounded by the billowing aroma from John Heinl's pipe as the old man reminisced to himself of happier days that only he must have been able to remember. As for Stiffy Green, his strange green eyes probably drooped pleasantly, closed over his crossed, stiff little paws on such frequent occasions.

It is said that man is the only creature with an awareness of its own mortality, and in this case, that notions seems to be born out in the strange behavior of Stiffy Green shortly after his cherished master succumbed to old age in 1921. Mr. Heinl was interred, unceremoniously but with many faithful acquaintances in attendance, in a conventional mausoleum and bid a fond farewell.

A neighboring family took control of the late Mr. Heinl's eccentric little pet, and did what they could to provide for it a decent new home. The story, however, was far from over.

Much to the amazement of his newly-adopted family, Stiffy Green began to mourn his missing master, and became a strangely despondent creature, refusing to eat, play, or do much of anything else but remain curled up in an agitated bundle by himself. It was a shock to the family, that never took into account the notion that a mere dumb animal could descend into depression.

And the situation only got worse, until one strange night, Stiffy Green must have heard the weird echo of His Master's Voice from somewhere beyond. He disappeared into the darkness, leaving the family frustrated as to his whereabouts, and searching for clues.

Working upon a hunch, the finally found their AWOL doggie pining away miserably in, you guessed it, Highland Lawn Cemetery, in front of the mausoleum of the departed Mr. Heinl. The dog was, aside from simply being inconsolable, also quite intelligent, as well.

They quickly reclaimed their pooch, bundling the stiff-legged little escapee back home, and doing their level best to see him happy and contented, once more. Alas, it was to no avail, for Stiffy found his way out of the house and to the cemetery once more, where he was interrupted in what had become for him an apparent vigil. It was the most perplexing conundrum the people had ever seen, and furthermore, must have left them feeling a bit put out since all their overtures of affection were insufficient to win the dog away from his dead former owner.

The central thing that so intrigued them though, and must, surely, at this point, be intriguing the reader was: How in the world did the animal KNOW where John Heinl was buried to begin with?

Whatever the solution to this particular puzzlement, after the third time the dog escaped to be found, yet again, at the door of the mausoleum at Highland Lawn, the family decided to, quietly, let Stiffy Green go about his business. They, in short, said, "To heck with it!" and let the dog stay there, in the cemetery where he so obviously belonged.

They were, however, a considerate family if nothing else, and so they took great pains to provide the animal food and water during the long hours of its self-enforced loneliness. The dog, meanwhile, stayed put, indefinitely, and eventually, seemed to come to some sort of strange, final resolution in his apparent thinking.

Whether because of grief, or out of an inborn desire toward suicide, Stiffy Green began to ignore food and water, and simply sat, ever ready to join his old master again, on the other side. The family that had at first experienced such joy at adopting him, looked on sadly as he began to, literally, waste away to nothing. By this time, the strange legend of a feral, devoted dog on a hunger strike against death, started to spread. Not a few locals came out to Highland Lawn to catch a glimpse of the old beast, but they were always greeted with a shallow bark and a fleeting glimpse before Stiffy used his last remaining strength to run and hide. Some said it was a legitimate wonder.

Of course, the slow suicide of Stiffy Green finally culminated in the adopted family finding the body of the animal, and now wondering what they could possibly do to memorialize such a rare, faithful, and altogether exceptional specimen of four-legged life. Finally they hit upon the notion, for good or ill, of having Stiffy stuffed.

It was a local taxidermist who did the hard part, and the weird green eyes that had lent Stiffy his peculiar surname were replaced by glass replicas; the body was put into the "stiff-legged" walking position for which the bulldog was most regionally famous, and the remains were then interred, where ought they be, in the mausoleum of John Heinl, whom Stiffy loved fiercely in life as well as death.

Of course, they became a sort of local curiosity in Tere Haute, where young lovers, cruising the cemetery as a "make-out joint," would scare themselves silly recounting the strange saga of the suicidal bulldog, and his eerie dedication to his departed keeper. A flashlight could be shined through the bars of the glass doors of the mausoleum, and invariably, the reflection of the beam would light the green glass eyes of Stiffy in an unsettling fashion.

The years, however, have proved that man and dog, inseparable in life, are inseparable in the afterlife, as well. Strange rumors have the pair walking still, with ghostly feet, a strange and poignant spectacle at sunset.

Some claim they can smell the thick aroma of old pipe tobacco near the mausoleum of John Heinl, or that they can a hear a strange, hollow bark cry out. One man, a cemetery worker, stated unequivocally that he heard a hollow bark follow him out of the cemetery one evening.

He was a man that was familiar with John Heinl, and he knew the bark as that of Stiffy Green.

The most astounding reports however, concern phenomenon that is considerably more frightening than smoke and noise. For, it is said, when the sun begins to dip bellow the horizon, and the trees blow gently with the breeze, shaking shadows out of their leaves, that the figure of an old man and an little stiff-legged dog are seen walking in the rose-colored shades that manifest themselves before twilight. They seem to be happy, content, once more, to be together. In death, they have found the companionship that meant so much to them in life, once again.

A Visitor at Flynn Home

The following story was related to me by a third party that wishes to remain anonymous. Since the institution that is being written of here folded many years ago, it is certain that no one could be troubled to check the accuracy of this particular tale. But my source in the matter is unimpeachable, and tell it I must.

On a hill, in Marion Indiana, is the boarded-up remnants of an old nursing home which we will call Flynn Home. That is not what the proper name of this establishment was, but that is what we shall call it, and in a moment, you will realize why.

Walking about the grounds of the place, today, you get an impression of how it must have looked over ten years ago, and how much the building itself has fallen into gross disrepair: The windows, those that aren't broken through vandalism, are boarded, and graffiti mars the façade of the building in several spots.

The hallways inside must echo with emptiness, and the thought that many elderly people met their final hours within these walls seems to give the casual visitor who may drive up the tree-shaded hill, a sense of eerie timelessness. The place overlooks the road like an age-worn sentinel, and the oldest part of it was built in the late nineteenth century.

Of course, a building such as this, even during the years of operation, gave rise to a great number of ghostly rumors, especially for nursing staff who were compelled to work in the oldest section of the building. Stories of chilling cold spots, weird singing and laughter, bizarre murmurings, and unearthly stenches were spoken of side by side with such unlikely phenomena as objects that vanished or moved on their own. Little wonder then, that so many employees found it unsettling to work, late at night, in the oldest area of the nursing home.

This particular story, however, has less to do with the goings on in the oldest section of the now abandoned facility, than what was occurring, with alarming regularity, in the break room of the place.

During the 1970s, when the smoking of marijuana was accepted as a new, chic alternative lifestyle, it was no surprise to find several employees of even a medical establishment that were bold enough to light up the stuff and puff away while they were at work. Flynn Home was no exception to this rule, and the night shift quickly became quite an opportune time for "getting high," even while on the job.

We cannot vouch for the way things are run today at nursing care establishments, having no experience in the area, but at this time, there were no closed-circuit cameras, and apparently no real supervision of the staff after the administration had all left for the day. Suffice it to say, the residents were not getting the best care that money could buy.

It was late one night, when the experiencer of my strange little tale was sitting in the break room with several other employees. At this time, according to the person that related the incident to me, no one had dared yet slip outside to smoke up, but several must have been contemplating it, when, all of a sudden, the door buzzer mysteriously went off.

One of the staff quickly got up from her seat to check who could be ringing at such an hour. She went to the door, looked out, and was surprised to see an elderly, white-haired old lady standing there, as if confused. Not knowing what else to do, and thinking that, perhaps, she might be a resident that had managed to become "locked out," she let the old woman enter, and was surprised when she walked right by her and down the hall, as if she knew, exactly, where it was she wanted to go. At this point, after getting a closer look at her, the employee that had just let her in was certain that she had never before laid eyes on her.

"Can I help you?" the employee called after her, but the elderly woman ignored her, and continued walking until she came to the back hall that led into the employee break room. There, she settled down in a chair, with several curious sets of eyes regarding her, warily.

"I know what goes on here," said the woman, not unkindly. "I think it is time for you all to stop and ask yourselves if what you're doing is right. The people here require your full attention, or someone is going to get hurt, very badly. What if you gave someone the wrong medication?"

The nursing care staff, at this point, was completely stunned and not the least little bit afraid. Who was this woman? Did she work for the State?

"You girls could all stand to read your Bibles, and get closer to the Lord. You know, operating under the influence of drugs while you're trying to take care of old, sick people, is not just a crime. It's a sin."

They then noticed how odd the woman looked; how her dress seemed to be out-of-date by at least several decades, and her face looked very pale, and almost too-white. Someone leaned forward in their chair, and asked, "Who are you?"

The woman smiled strangely, got up, and walked back out of the break room door. The assembled employees listened in stunned silence as her footfalls rang down the hallway, and only a few seconds later the woman that had originally let her in, walked out after her, only to find that, in her amazement, the woman had disappeared.

Of course, the strange thing about that was, that there was no where for the woman to have been able to disappear to. No car pulled out of the parking lot that night, and no one drove away into the darkness, whatever may have occasioned her strange visit.

Needless to say, after this the employees ceased to smoke dope on the premises of the nursing home, and were left only with the puzzling feeling that they had been visited by someone that was not, strictly speaking, part of the natural order of things.

It was only later, when a particularly curious employee began digging through the history of the old home, that she happened upon a picture in the archives of the local library. It depicted the staff of the nursing home, standing in a group portrait, to celebrate the opening of the establishment. Standing in the front row, unmistakably, was the woman that had visited to sternly lecture the women that bizarre evening; the woman who stepped, seemingly, out of nowhere for a few minutes, and then disappeared. That woman had seemed to be in her mid-forties, and so did the woman in the photo that bore her uncanny likeness.

The opening of the nursing home was sometime in the late 1890's.

Return of the Gipper

George Gipp was a large, seemingly feckless young man who never properly graduated from high school. Yet, he lives on, today, in the memory of millions of football fans that remember him, chiefly, as the legendary "Gipper," the athletic phenomenon that featured as the subject of the classic American movie, Knute Rockne: All American, starring the late President Ronald Reagan.

George was, by all accounts, an unruly boy who spent his days playing pool in seedy dives, and wondering what in the world he was going to do with the rest of his life. He had always been a great athlete, excelling in baseball while merely sliding through his classes by managing to do as little actual academic work as possible. In that sense, he was not unlike millions of other boys of his age, who gravitate to rough games and shirk school as being somehow "for sissies."

George's life, however, was to take a radical turn, for it was not long after high school that the young idler chanced upon an encounter with an old friend, an individual that had graduated from Notre Dame University in Indiana, and was now playing in the semi-professional leagues. Knowing full well Georges' physical prowess, this man suggested he apply to Notre Dame for a baseball scholarship. Although, at first, the young man was reticent to leave his carefree lifestyle, he was eventually persuaded to board a train to Elkhart, a train that would eventually lead him to Notre Dame and national acclaim.

George was ensconced at Washington Hall, a dormitory presided over by Catholic Brothers, and loafed his way through classes in his first semester. Feeling like a fish out of water due to his slightly older age, George exhibited the same lethargic "devil may care" attitude that he had at home in Michigan, the attitude that had soured his last years in high school, assuring a poor academic performance.

It was one day, while playing football with some friends, he was noticed by none other than the fabled Knute Rockne, football coach for the Fighting Irish. Rockne immediately knew talent when he saw it, and, approaching the young man, asked him if he had ever played high school football.

"No, baseball is my game."

"Put on a uniform tomorrow and come out with the football scrubs. I think you'll make a great player."

Gipp, not particularly fond of football, did as he was instructed, and went out the next day to try out for the Fighting Irish. It quickly became apparent to all involved that he was an electrifying, masterful player, who seemed born to the pantheon of gridiron gods.

It was four sterling years for college football, and George "The Gipper" Gipp lead his team to twenty consecutive victories and two Western Championships, playing both offense and defense, and his name quickly became a byword for athletic excellence and rugged, sportsmanlike struggle. It was all too much for the young man from Michigan, and his meteoric rise to college football greatness spurred his not-inconsiderable ego and his brash demeanor to new heights.

He ruffled the feathers of Brother Maurilius, who oversaw the boys dormitory where Gipp was living. One night, when Gipp had failed to return before curfew from a night on the town, Brother Maurilius confronted him, telling him that it was the last time he would flagrantly violate the rules. Brother Mauritius threatened young George with disciplinary actions—actions that would, most certainly, disqualify him from participating in the school sports program.

The Gipper was horrified, and was careful to come back to the dorm before curfew afterwards. He was so leery of the threats issued by Brother Marilius that one weekend night, coming home from a party, he was aghast to realize the he was, most definitely, going to be late. It was only a few minutes to midnight, and he knew that once he got there, the doors would be locked, and all he could do to get inside would be to wake Brother Mauritius, who would be furious. Mariulius would , almost certainly, write him up for disciplinary suspension, and his football playing would be over.

It was a chilly night, but not so chilly that George Gipp was willing to risk the wrath of Brother Maurilius. Instead, he slept that night on the steps of Washington Hall. According to legend, this is what occasioned the illness that was to later rob college football of one of its all-time heroes.

Gipp began to develop a sore throat and cough, and, in time, it was discovered that he had pneumonia. Although he struggled on practicing for a short while, Rockne quickly forced the young man to see a doctor. It was only a short amount of time later that his condition worsened.

It was in November of 1920 that George Gipp, after leading his team in a winning game against Northwestern University, finally became too ill to continue to play. Admitted to St. Joseph's Hospital, Gipp lingered on in a miserable condition while reporters and sports fans waited with baited breath for news of his recovery. Alas, it was not meant to be.

By December 12 of 1920, the man was literally, on the edge of death. His family and coach was summoned, and George motioned Rockne to his side, telling him, "I've got to go, Rock. It's all right. I'm not afraid. Some time Rock, when the team's up against it, when things are wrong and the breaks are beating the boys—tell them to go in there with all they've got and win one for the Gipper. I don't know where I'll be then Rock, but I'll know about it and I'll be happy."

It was two days later that George "The Gipper" Gipp died. He was laid to rest on December 17, 1920, in a funeral attended by the entire student body and a multitude of fans, family, friends, and supporters. It was truly a milestone in the history of Notre Dame, and a time of great grief for many people. Gipp was only twenty-five years old at the time of death.

Meanwhile, life at Washington Hall resumed much as it has before George Gipp ever set foot within. However, it was only a short time later that strange reports began to surface from some of the students, reports of the bizarre sound of musical instruments that seemingly played themselves, and the unearthly groan that seemed to creep across the corridors of Washington Hall in the dead of night.

Trumpeter Jim Clancy, late one night when he was practicing in the band room, was astonished that, when he stopped playing, he could still hear a bizarre sound coming from a corner of the room. It sounded like grunting, and, upon approaching the corner, he was shocked to find that, even though it sat lonely on the floor with no one manipulating it, the great tuba apparently had taken a mind of its own and was now playing itself!

This was enough to convince the young man that something strange was afoot, and he quickly got himself out of the there. At first he told no one of his strange experience, fearing correctly that he wouldn't be believed, but it was only a short time later that other students began to have their own encounters with the eerie noises, and not a few of them were present when doors slammed of their own accord, footsteps and weird groaning came echoing down the halls, and personal items would disappear and reappear in the strangest places and under the oddest of circumstances.

It was all too much for Brother Marsilius, who did what he could to quell an outbreak he saw as nothing more than juvenile pranks and "mass hysteria." But still the strange footsteps and weird happenings continued, and progressed.

One incident, recounted in Mark Merriman's excellent book, School Spirits, has the ghost of George Gipp riding a phantom steed up the steps of Washington Hall, and disappearing through the doorway! While we concede that spirits may have actually been involved in this puzzling scenario, we cannot altogether be sure exactly what spirits and where they were purchased or consumed.

Even Brother Marsilius had to admit himself baffled when, one night while lying in bed he heard a horrific sound that was "somewhere between a crash and an explosion." Running in panic from his room, he went out onto the landing, looking wildly around for some explanation for the noise that had just awakened him from sleep. Of course, in the entire building there was found nothing to account for the strange sounds, nor was any explanation forthcoming, except that several students, disdainful of Brother Marsilius' disbelief, had conspired to play a late night gag at his expense.

Due to the strange, carnivalesqe atmosphere the place acquired during those first heady days of the discovery, a skeptical professor led a contingent of eager pupils to spend the night in the old band room, to try and ferret out if there was actually any truth to the rumors being told. It was not long before the professor and his group of young adventurers settled down for the night, however, that one of them was, apparently, tossed from his folding cot by unseen hands. Immediately after this, a bizarre glowing eminence was said to be seen, briefly, in a corner of the room. This was accompanied by wailing, and such a traumatic feeling of unease that the little group found themselves unable to continue with the ex periment, and departed in fright that night.

Of course, after Brother Marsilius' own experience, he clamored to his superiors and demanded that something be done. An exorcism was surely called for, but, whether or not one was ever actually performed by any member of the Order of the Holy Cross is strictly a matter of conjecture. If one was performed, however, it seems not to have been overwhelmingly successful.

Over the decades, a steady stream of reports have continued to emerge from those who have set foot and lingered in the creaky old passageways of Washington Hall. Students have reported the same wailing moans, cold spots, the slamming of doors by invisible hands, and the same strange feelings of being ogled or watched, year after year. One man claimed to have felt the ghost touch his shoulder as he walked upstairs, while another has spoken of the bizarre, misty illumination that sometimes lingers too long in the darkness.

Has "The Gipper" come home from beyond the grave, to walk like a prisoner through the dark corridors of Washington Hall, year after year, decade after decade, quietly watching over the comings and goings of those who are young and filled with the energy and promise of a life he can never again know?

Who knows? However, what is for certain is that Washington Hall is never fully empty. When spring gives way to summer, and students begin filing out to experience youth and life and love in their own way, there is a lingering energy they leave behind. And it is that energy, embodied in the sum total of all of our fears of the unknown, that gives life to tales and experiences such as these.

Old County Jail

J ails, and most especially prisons, are frightening and
spiritually desolate places by their very nature. No one
who has ever been confined in jail would tell you that they
enjoyed it, and fewer still would ever want to return to
that place once they had left.

Yet, jail is one of the defining institutions of our civilization, and the idea that those who trespass against our
laws and values must be confined and kept apart from the
rest of society is what prevents our world from degenerat-
ing into brutal anarchy.

Within the walls of an old jail, one senses that there
must, indeed, reside some of the pent-up misery and
brutality that has existed within the confines of brick,
mortar, and steel. One wonders if, in the dead of night,
an ancient and abandoned jail does not echo with the
misery of days gone by. According to visitors of Old
County Jail, in Valparaiso, Indiana, that is exactly what
occurs.

Old County Jail was built in 1865, and went through
an incredible amount of renovation and expansion during the decades of its activity. It was originally built as a
home for the Porter County Sheriff, but in time, facilities
were expanded to include a handful of inmates. As the
community began to grow, it later boasted sections for
women and juveniles, the mentally deranged, as well as
hardened toughs that needed to be held in more secure
confinements. During the final years of operation, the
Old County Jail was a veritable sardine can, having at

one point one hundred criminals crammed within a space meant for only thirty-five.

According to author Mark Merriman, in his book Haunted Indiana 4, Porter County soon saw fit to put the old, insufficient jail out of commission, and instead built themselves a new, bright, modern facility that is still in use. The Old County Jail was soon turned into the Porter County Historical Museum, and this is where our story really begins to pick up speed.

For, it was not long before the museum employees began to get the creeping notion that there were still a few inmates being held behind the walls of the Old County Jail, and that death itself had refused them a parole.

The initial evidence of unearthly inmates came via the strange sound of "skipping stones" from the floors above, in the area where the jail cells had been. Intrigued and baffled, museum personnel investigated, but, to their amazement, could find no source for the annoying ruckus.

It was not until later, when happenstance brought an elderly guard and one of the museum employees together, that the startled persons who had first heard the skipping learned of the jail custom of skipping small stones back and forth between cells, with small notes attached, as a means of communication.

As chilling as that revelation was, it was only the first in a long series of bizarre antics. The weird sounds of banging metal, hushed whispers, and even a sickened human groan, have been heard, and have even followed visitors and workers at Old County Jail around while they are walking on the premises. Objects, such as two stones used, obviously, for "skipping notes" back and forth between cells, have appeared, disappeared, and reappeared without explanation, and there have even been times when the employees have left the premises in a hurry late at night. All the better to be away before the voices start, or some other manifestation forces them to ponder occurrences they would rather not think about.

One bizarre occurrence, though, is far more frightening than all the rest combined. Related by one Mrs. Schmitt, it involves the dark apparition of a strange man.

One day, while preparing a meeting room during daylight hours, Mrs. Schmitt glanced at the long end of a table, and to her amazement, sitting upright in an old chair she could see the shadowy figure of a man begin to materialize. It was a strange, misty figure—indistinct, but Mrs. Schmitt found herself so overcome with terror that she quickly left the room.

Of course, it is not only the workers at the Old County Jail that have experienced the strange goings-on, visitors to the Old County Jail have reported the presence of several spirits, including that of a young lady in an old-fashioned dress who walks through the hallways downstairs. Many visitors assumed, at first, that this was simply an employee in costume. Of course, when they were made aware that there was no such employee, they were rightfully mystified.

There are supposedly the spirits of a child and a delightful dog (whose presumed earthly remains are displayed nearby) running around the grounds as well. It is said that the dog can be heard at night, barking loudly, and this has been reported by custodial staff. Some visitors have also claimed they can "feel" a weird brushing against their legs at times, as if a small invisible dog was loose in the darkened hallways, seeking attention.

The many artifacts that make up the collection at the Old County Jail have, like many such old objects, bizarre energy connected to them. One such item, a bullet-riddled World War I helmet, caused quite an interesting anecdote in the life of a curator who happened to take the helmet from the museum as part of a demonstration he was giving at various schools concerning the period.

Leaving the helmet in his home over a weekend proved to be the most unsettling thing he could have done, for it was not many hours before he started noticing bizarre "flashes" of light out of the corners of his eyes. These mysterious flashes seemed to follow him around the house, and appeared especially vividly as he lay down to sleep in the darkness of his bedroom.

He also began to feel an odd sense of presence around him at night as he lay in bed, and he quickly decided to take the helmet back to the museum where it belonged. As he was sitting in his office telling a co-worker of his bizarre experiences, he found himself running his hands over the helmet. Suddenly, as his fingers touched the bullet holes in the side of the helmet, he found himself recoiling in pain.

The surface of the object, for some unknown reason, had become hot. His fingers were, in fact, burned and began to blister.

There have been other reports by museum workers of seeing a strange man, who appears as an indistinct shade, his body tapering off into darkness and mist. One worker recalled an incident with an antique typewriter whose keys could not be sufficiently manipulated.

After several minutes, the typewriter was laid down upon a filing cabinet while the operating manual was consulted. Imagine the surprise of the museum staff person when they suddenly began to hear the clack-clack sound of several keys apparently typing themselves.

One young intern also reported the appearance, three times in a single evening, of a woman in a flowing white gown. While preparing the Old County Jail for a visit by a local chapter of the Ghost Trackers, he was walking through the parlor area when he saw the strange ghost staring at him, standing by a window.

Thinking he was merely imagining things, he proceeded to the kitchen, where he set about making coffee, but was alarmed when he felt as if someone entered and slipped an arm around his waist. Turning quickly, he looked out the doorway into the darkness, certain he could see the dark figure of the woman standing in the hallway, staring at him. His nerves on edge now, he quickly moved from the kitchen and back out through the parlor. Looking up at the stairwell as he passed, he was shocked to, once again, see the shadow figure of the woman in the white gown.

Of course, the strange woman has been sighted by several different witnesses over the years. One man, whose job it was to open the building in the morning, was greeted by an ominous sight the moment he stepped into the parlor and into the deep must of the old place. That morning, he got what, to date, has been the most detailed description of the strange, female spirit that walks the grounds of the Porter County Historical Museum.

She was standing in the dining room area, dressed in an old fashioned dress, and with a short coat and Victorian hat. Whether or not she was aware of the man's presence or not, he became instantly aware of hers. He spent the rest of the morning sitting out on the stoop by himself, waiting for his co-workers to arrive.

Who knows what shadows and echoes of the past still reverberate through he darkened place far into the wee hours of the morning. Those in the know recount strange, muffled conversations in empty rooms, and the persistent feeling that some of the luckless inmates of Old County Jail are still serving a very long sentence.

The Spirits of Story

Story, Indiana is a town that exists, like a lonely sentinel, on the virtual cusp between past and future. It was built by Dr. George Story in 1851, from a land grant given him by President Millard Fillmore, and in only a short amount of time it grew to nearly eclipse the nearby town of Nashville as a center of trading and commerce. The town became a bustling little place, spanning nine buildings and twenty-three acres, and its central attraction was the popular Story Inn.

Sadly, the town of Story would soon fall on tough times. After years of progressing upward at a steady pace, the town finally succumbed to the economic pulls of the Great Depression. As residents started heading out to look for some means of securing their livelihood, the once lively streets of Story, Indiana began to grow dark and silent, until all that was left was the general store and a quaint collection of crumbling buildings, rotting in the wind.

It was not until many years later, under the entrepreneurial aegis of a struggling couple, that the old general store was purchased and refurbished into an elegant restaurant and hotel. At last, a little of the rustic charm of the old Story, Indiana began to creep through. Later, in the mid-1990s, the property changed hands once again, and the new owners, both wealthy gentleman in their own right, set out to restore the classic community to a semblance of its former self. In time, the Story Inn opened its door to visitors once more, and that is when the truly interesting events began to transpire.

Visitors to the Story Inn began to leave their own personal accounts of visitations by the mysterious "Blue Lady," a phantom that appears in the guest rooms upstairs, often at the foot of a sleeping couple's bed. Though some of these accounts were very much tongue-in-cheek, many of them related incidents that were startlingly similar.

The name of the Blue Lady was coined by the new owners of Story, who happened to find a mysterious blue portrait in an attic that seemed to fit the description of the ghost. The image of the ghost became well known, and burned into the memory of anyone that has ever had an experience with the Blue Lady.

One such woman reported seeing the Blue Lady one day as she was sitting in a rocking chair, looking out the glass of the back door. Suddenly, she could see the image of a face begin to crystallize in the glass, and she knew immediately, who it was. Of course, there was no one standing behind her, and no explanation for the face in the glass. The woman later described the eyes of the Blue Lady as "hypnotic," and "piercing."

Often the Blue Lady is accompanied by the strong smell of perfume, and an icy feeling of being watched. Visitors to Story have reported waking up and knowing that someone was in the room with them. On one occasion, the bizarre presence was made manifest in a most unusual and striking way.

Two guests of the Inn, who were occupying the Blue Lady Room (as it has come to be known), had just settled in for the evening, when the all too familiar scent of roses seemed to waft, cloyingly, in the suddenly chilly air. The husband, who had been in the bathroom brushing his teeth, suddenly came out complaining that his wife had turned on the air conditioning. When she assured him she had not, he remained insistent that he had felt a cold blast of air grip him, as if "something freezing brushed past me." Later that night, while the couple lay in bed, the wife awoke in a grip of fear, and said that she could smell the distinct smell of a heavy breath full of roses being blasted into her face.

Of course, equally disturbing was the tendency for an upstairs door (leading out to a balcony), to suddenly swing open and shut of its own accord. Lest any of our readers get the mistaken impression that this was caused by a shifting of the old building, or even the wind, it should be noted that the door not only moved of its own accord, but also managed to unlock itself on several occasions.

Curiously, heavy pictures have been known to fly from the walls, and glasses have been known to mysteriously shatter at the dining room tables in the restaurant below. Several workmen recount an odd tale that transpired one day while they were taking a break from their labors.

One of the workmen was pitching a rubber ball, when, accidentally, his ball bounced down into the darkness of the basement stairs. He started down to retrieve it when he and his fellow co-workers were alerted by the sound of rubber thumping against the wooden stairs.

The ball skipped back up the stairs, according to the men, and came to rest at the foot of its owner.

The employees at the Story Inn are well-aware of the strange voices, the weird mumbling, and the footsteps that sound out quietly, in the dark. They have, apparently, become use to these things, and various employees have confessed that they feel the Story Inn to be a "secure" or "protected" place, and that the Blue Lady, whether she really exists or not, at the very least makes their job a little more eventful and interesting. She has been suspected of helping the employees in a variety of strange ways, including making coffee, and turning on the building heat in the morning before anyone else arrives.

It should be noted that the Story Inn is not the only supposedly haunted building in Story, but that the Old Doc Story House is also said to be inhabited by a resident spirit. This particular ghost is known for being gentle, for politely "pinching" guests, for watching over the premises, and infusing the old rooms, strangely, with the heavy scent of old cherry pipe tobacco. He waits, like any spirit, in the habitations that so comforted him in life.

Just what he is waiting for, no one on this side of the grave can ever say for certain.

The Faceless Nun

Foley Hall was a great stone edifice that dated back to 1860, when St. Mary of the Woods College in Terre Haute was first founded in the wilds of Central Indiana by nuns that had journeyed from France to found a religious commune in the wooded areas of the New World. Though the idea of religious and educational instruction strictly for women must have seemed strange to the rugged settlers that pioneered Indiana territory, the Sisters struggled for decades, until they became a viable and bustling religious community and a cultural center amid the rough hewn prairie people.

The story of the "Faceless Nun" is a legend that goes far back in the history of the school. The story is simple, yet elegant and poignant.

There was once a young nun at St. Mary's whose greatest pleasure was in painting. She diligently studied art, and her ability to transmit an image to canvass was unparalleled. Thus, it was not long before she was teaching art classes at the school herself, delighting the sisters with portraits of them as they went about their daily activities and chores.

So accomplished an artist was she, that it was finally suggested that she make the next logical leap in testing her own talent, and attempt to do a portrait of her own likeness.

Intrigued with the prospect of this, the young novitiate set up her canvass in the studio at Foley Hall, and began to carefully paint herself while looking at her reflection in a highly-polished mirror. She began the work in earnest, but, as she proceeded, she could see that, without a doubt, it would reflect an excellence hitherto unknown in many of her portraits. It might, she conceded to her fellow nuns, be her finest work.

Of course, it may have been the sin of pride that proved her fatal undoing. For, even though she had adequately filled in the entire canvass with detailed precision, she found herself, somehow, unaccountably blocked as it came time to finish the most important part of any portrait—the face. She lapsed into a kind of nervous lethargy, unsure of her ability to capture the essential spark of life that is the essence of any painted image. She gave herself a short respite from her efforts, but it proved to be, altogether, the wrong thing to do.

Possibly through the sheer strain of her efforts, (which found her, incidentally, working by gaslight all night and literally falling asleep over her work at times) the young nun fell ill, dying only several days later. Perhaps this was the result of an epidemic, a not uncommon occurrence in the late Victorian Era, or maybe it was just sheer exhaustion, but, whatever the case, the self-portrait stood as her uncompleted final piece. In time, it was taken from the art studio of Foley Hall, put into a storage closet, and forgotten.

What came next, however, was truly interesting, as the legend of a strange, "faceless" nun began to circulate among the students who walked through the darkened passages of Foley Hall, stories that could not be easily dismissed. Whether or not the legend came first, or if it was the strange encounters that actually led to the weaving of the familiar tale, no one can now say. What is undeniable, however, is the presence of the Faceless Nun, who walked the dim hallways of Foley Hall, a forlorn reminder of a life and incredible talent cut short before they even bloomed.

The best anecdotes concerning the Faceless Nun came from none other than a fellow Sister and teacher at St. Mary's, the art professor Sister Esther, who before her death related some of the following anecdotes and history of the Faceless Nun to a local reporter.

Although Foley Hall had always had an aura about it that seemed to invite suspicions of the ghostly, it was not until one night, while Sister Esther was working late on a particularly pressing project, that she became aware of a presence in the room with her. Feeling uneasy, she went outside of her own room, going down the hall to an adjacent studio, where she saw a young woman standing outside the door, looking disturbed.

"Whatever could be the matter?" asked Sister Esther, noting the strange, nervous look on the young student's face.

The girl looked at her strangely, and then said, "It's that young Sister. She has been in and out of the room all night, yet every time I speak to her she says nothing. And I can never seem to get a look at her face."

Surprised, Sister Esther went into the room to investigate, but found nothing. The description of the young nun matched no one that Sister Esther had ever heard of before, but she was alarmed to say the least. It was only a short time later, however, that the faceless young sister began to make more frequent appearances at the school.

One day, Sister Esther was lecturing in her class when, as she was standing in front of a student's desk, she was surprised to see the girl lift her head, say something over her shoulder, and then jerk her head about as if surprised.

The girl said, "Are you everywhere? You were just standing beside me, weren't you?"

As odd as this particular happening was, it paled in comparison to the night that Sister Esther was called down to the art studio by a disturbed young student. As the young woman stood at the canvas, she stated emphatically that, "There is someone else in the room with us. She is over in the corner. She is dressed like one of the old time Sisters, and I can't seem to get a look at her face."

Sister Esther stood there, incredulously, as the student described the strange, mournful figure in black. Sister Esther learned later that the student was, generally, considered to be a "sensitive" that could see and feel many things that ordinary people could not.

She continued to describe the strange form that she saw, even beginning to sketch it, as the invisible phantom walked over to an old closet, and dissolved into the doorway. Sister Esther realized, suddenly, that the room was freezing.

Disturbing accounts of the Faceless Nun continued to come from a variety of students, so many, in fact, that Foley Hall became a place on campus to consciously avoid. Most students refused to be inside the hall at night, and those that were forced to, for whatever reason, often found themselves inventing excuses to not linger in the place as the sun began to dip below the trees. Many students would, in time, come to assert that they, too, had occasion to run into the Faceless Nun, and many complained of the eerie feelings and icy cold sensations of gloom that Foley Hall gave them.

It was a short time later that Sister Esther went to her superiors, and a special Mass was commenced, ostensibly to quiet the restless ghost of the Faceless Nun. Though this seems to have had some positive impact, it didn't squelch the weird phenomena completely, and students from time to time still reported seeing the alarming image of a weeping nun, whose face seems always to somehow elude the observations of the witness.

It was several years later that Foley Hall was torn down. Whither went the spirit of the Faceless Nun, no one can say, but we can well imagine that that tormented soul lives on, in some capacity. Perhaps she still wanders the lonely grounds, looking out from beneath a dark hood, with eyes that see everything and nothing, all at once.

Part two

Stories by

Jonathan Titchenal

White River Boulevard

Traditionally, haunted houses and haunted house stories are not invasive. Most spirits, especially those who haunt houses over a long period, do not interact with the living. The apparition that walks every night along the same corridor does not see the people who see it. Whoever or whatever it is, the ghost is clearly not on the same material plane. This has given rise to a host of theories about whether ghosts are sentient beings. Many people believe ghosts are nothing more than residual energy from an earlier event, replaying an echo of itself over and over again. Others have suggested that it is the presence of a living person that causes the effect, and that sensitive people and psychics are able to look through an occasional window in time. If this is true, then ghosts themselves have no substance of any kind.

But what can you say when the focus of the haunting is not on the house, but on the occupant?

When I began research for this book, I initially looked for older legends about Indiana hauntings. A modern appraisal of old stories seemed the best course for my section of the narrative. Just two weeks into my research, I was contacted by a young woman—who I will identify as S.—who had heard that Tom Baker and I were hunting up ghosts, and she claimed she was part of an active haunting in the city of Muncie. I wrote back asking for more information, and she replied with her story.

Eight months prior to our meeting, she had moved into an older apartment complex off of White River

Boulevard. The disturbances began immediately afterward. She would wake in the night to find a shadowy figure perched at the edge of the bed. This figure would be watching her intently, sometimes peering down into her face so that she felt it was only inches away. She experienced a distinct sense of menace from the figure, and she would reach for the bedside table to turn on the lamp. By the time she did this, the apparition would be gone, but the sense of malice would remain, even with the lights on.

As the days went on, the disturbances grew steadily worse, until she would sometimes see figures moving out of the corner of her eye in the light of day. Objects that were in plain sight would go missing and never be found. Footsteps and banging noises from other areas of the apartment would wake her in the night, and her sleep was suffering because of it. She had been forced, she told me, to cover up her dresser mirror. According to her, things kept wandering around in the reflected bedroom at night.

I was initially dubious about the story. I had trouble imagining an apartment being haunted, since my own apartment seemed sterile and blank in comparison to a house or public building. The shadowy figure at the foot of the bed was a common occurrence in night terrors (panic attacks from sudden waking), as well as nightmares where the afflicted person has difficulty waking up. The brain produces a chemical that keeps the body from moving while we sleep, and sometimes this chemical doesn't leave the body immediately. People wake up and find themselves paralyzed for several seconds, unable to move or speak. In many cases, people claim to see a shadowy figure standing near the bed. The reason for this has never been explained, but the two experiences seem to go hand in hand. I agreed to meet in person with S to discuss her story and investigate the apartment.

We met in Muncie, not far from her apartment, and I took a moment to review what she had told me. I was immediately impressed by her level-headedness. She had never experienced anything even remotely like this before, she told me. Her retelling of the events was clinical and straightforward. She told me she was living alone. She was a graduate student at a nearby university, and had little time for friends or company. She couldn't recall any instances where visitors had mentioned anything out of the ordinary. I asked if I could look around the apartment, and she agreed. Together we drove down White River Boulevard to her complex.

Her apartment was a narrow, cramped, L-shaped space in an older building. The building itself was showing signs of wear and tear, and S told me that her landlord did not respond to maintenance calls. There was only one bedroom, a long hallway leading to the living room, and an attached kitchen. On first impression, the apartment seemed claustrophobic and restricted, but not sinister. Light came in through the sliding glass doors in the living room, though I saw no other windows. S gave me a tour of the living room, kitchen, and bedroom areas, pointing out where events had happened as she went. There were no inconsistencies in her story, and nothing to make me suspect she was embellishing her experiences. When the tour had finished, I asked what I could do for her, and what she wanted out of the investigation.

She was interested in having proof that her experiences were not solitary. If whatever was happening was due to her alone, it might mean there was something wrong with her mind, and she would continue to worry. If the events were due to an outside force, and they happened to others, it would mean that she wasn't hallucinating. As frightening as the prospect of a malicious outside entity was, she was more afraid of a creeping dysfunction in her own mind.

I asked if it would be possible for me to spend a night alone in the apartment, and we set up a time during the weekend when she would be visiting family. We exchanged contact information, and I agreed to come by and get her apartment key on the upcoming Friday. I thanked her for her time, and we parted ways.

That Friday, I picked up the apartment keys and moved my equipment into the living room. I am not a professional investigator, and my monitoring equipment is audio and visual only. I would be relying on my own senses for the bulk of my information. I bid S goodbye and set up the audio recorder and camera to monitor the hallway and the bedroom. Once everything was in place, I sat down in the living room and passed the time reading. It was evening by this point, and the sun was shining through the sliding doors. I decided not to turn on any of the lights yet, and read by the sunlight for some time. When the light grew dim, I put the book down and leaned back in the recliner, listening to the apartment. It was quiet and still, except for the small noises that older buildings make as they settle. I heard nothing and saw nothing. At some point, I must have fallen asleep.

I have tried to be accurate in recounting what happened next, but a great deal of what I experienced was not physical. Just as people can often tell when something bad is happening without obvious sensory input, I believe there are many levels of perception we do not yet understand.

I was awakened by a tap on my shoulder. I jumped to my feet and looked around, but saw nothing. By this time, twilight had come, and the room was very dark. I had been dubious about the sense of malice S had described, but at that moment I felt it, and understood what she had meant. A sense of being watched filled the room, and the hate in that watchful presence was very real. I began to feel that I was in danger of being harmed in some way. My instincts won over my professionalism, and I hurried to turn the light on.

I was surprised to find that S had been right on another count, as the sense of malice and attention did not fade with the lights on. I resolved to stay the rest of the night, but I found it very difficult to concentrate on anything and impossible to sleep. I would catch myself turning around to make sure there was no one behind me. Throughout the night, I caught movement from the corners of my eyes with the lights turned on, but saw nothing directly. The sense of menace did not dissolve until well into the next morning.

When S arrived, I returned her keys to her and reported my findings. The camera and the tape recorder had caught nothing out of the ordinary, but my own account seemed to be enough to satisfy her. Despite the prospect of returning to an apartment with a malevolent spirit, she seemed relieved and thanked me for my time. When the time came to put this book together, I contacted her for a follow-up report, but she informed me that she had moved out of the apartment building. By all accounts, her new apartment is free of disturbances.

Much of what I experienced at the White River Boulevard apartment I could reasonably explain as my own imagination and nerves. I don't believe this was the case, but I have no way of proving it, even to myself. I know that the room was filled by an unseen presence, and I know that presence directed a great deal of hate at me, but I have no rational way of explaining it. Neither did S.

What I cannot find is a way of explaining is the tap on the shoulder that woke me. It was completely real and physical. When I stood up, I expected a person to be standing behind me. If everything else is invalid, where then did this very physical impression come from? I cannot consider this aspect of the experience without believing the rest of my impressions to be at least possible.

While my investigation was not conclusive, I believe the case of White River Boulevard to be a genuine haunting. It is one of the few times I have been startled enough to break my own guidelines, and it stands out in my memory as a singularly frightening event.

The Slippery Noodle Inn

Many people make the mistake of assuming haunt-ings only occur in lonely or isolated places. When we think of haunted houses, the image that comes to mind first is often a lonely country manor, or some abandoned farmhouse. The truth is that hauntings occur in the city just as often as in the lonely places of the world. Cities are high-density areas where scores of people live and love and die, and over the years, the buildings that survive tend to be pretty interesting places.

The Slippery Noodle Inn, in Indianapolis, is one of those places. While a bar doesn't immediately lend itself to the idea of ghostly disturbances, more than one specter has been reported in and around the old establishment.

The Slippery Noodle is the oldest bar in Indiana. It was originally founded, way back in 1850, as the Tremont House. It was run as a roadhouse- where people could stay the night, and was one of the first German clubs in the Indianapolis area. In the 1860s, it was known as the Concordia House, after the name of the German immigrant ship. It later became Germania House, and remained Germania House until World War I, when the owner changed its name to Beck's Saloon for political reasons. Later, Walter Moore purchased the saloon and called it Moore's Beer Tavern, until prohibition caused him to rename it as Moore's Restaurant. When prohibi-tion was over, it was Moore's Beer Tavern again, and it remained so for many years.

In 1963, the bar was bought by Harold and Loren Yeagy, and named The Slippery Noodle Inn, for reasons which have never been especially clear. The bar remained in the possession of the Yeagys, and was passed to Harold's son in 1985. In recent years, it has garnered a reputation as an excellent blues club, and it is well known in the Indianapolis area.

It's no surprise that there are spooks haunting the Inn. It was part of the Underground Railroad during Civil War days, and at one point there was an operating bordello on the grounds. Interestingly enough, the bordello years came to an end when one of the patrons was murdered. The Brady and Dillinger gangs also made use of the Inn during prohibition, and the basement was once a slaughterhouse for swine and cattle.

The basement, in particular, is said to be haunted. There have been several reports by the management of an older African American man appearing in the basement area. This may have had something to do with the Inn's days as part of the Underground Railroad, though no one has recognized the man, so far as we know. Other activity, though none so specific as the man in the basement, has been reported in different parts of the building, including the portion which was once the brothel. Supposedly the ghostly remains of the ladies who once worked the building are none too pleased by intrusive strangers, especially men. Reports have claimed that doors on the top story open and shut of their own accord, and many female apparitions have been sighted.

I was able to get in contact with a resident of Indianapolis named Debra Rhea, and we spoke at length concerning the Inn:

JT: Thank you for talking with me about this.

DR: No problem.

JT: When we spoke earlier, you said you'd spent some time at the Slippery Noodle.

DR: Yeah, I used to go down there on Friday and Saturday nights sometimes, after work. I knew a lot of people who went there.

JT: And you saw things there?

DR: Ghosts, you mean?

JT: Yes.

DR: I don't know. I think so. I mean, sometimes when I stayed late I saw things. My friend, Adam, said he saw something there once or twice too. It's really common. I've heard a lot of stories.

JT: Are there any other reports you know of?

DR: Oh yeah. The staff has all sorts of stories about it. They say they see things all the time.

JT: And what did you see?

DR: Well, this was about a year ago. I remember one night I was there late, and I saw someone walk by out of the corner of my eye. I was facing the other way, and they were off to the side, where no one was around. It wasn't anything special, but I just saw someone go by; but I got a funny feeling, and I turned around, and there was no one there.

JT: What did they look like?

DR: I didn't get a good look. I think it was a man, pretty tall, dark hair. There's no way he could have walked away. He just was gone.

JT: What was he wearing?

DR: Um. It looked like a suit, I think. Probably a suit. I just got a feeling that something wasn't right—you know, and I looked over, and there was no one.

JT: Did you ever see anything else?

DR: I saw things out of the corner of my eye sometimes, when it was quieter there. I saw other people do it too sometimes. I'd just get that feeling that something wasn't right, that something else was going on. It was weird.

JT: Were you ever frightened by it?

DR: Um, I don't think it was ever frightening. It was weird and different, and that could be kind of frightening, but I didn't ever think anything would hurt me. I never felt like that.

JT: Do you believe the Slippery Noodle is haunted, then?

DR: Oh yeah, definitely. I believe in ghosts, and I think they can, you know, sort of cross paths with people sometimes. I think that happens a lot in some places.

JT: And this is one of those places?

DR: Definitely. Yeah.

Though I have yet to experience anything personally, I have come to the conclusion that the Slippery Noodle Inn is the genuine article. Some hauntings interact with people, or have a definite purpose. Others are quiet, long-time hauntings, accumulated over the years as humanity interacts with a building. These types of activity are reported so frequently, we can't help but assume some connection between human beings and ghosts. What still remains a mystery is whether the line is direct, and all spirits are human shades, or whether the world of the supernatural is as strange and convoluted as it seems to be to the living.

Regardless, the Slippery Noodle is more than just a haunted building, and we suggest that travelers to the Indianapolis area should stop by, listen to some fine blues, and have a beer.

And keep your eyes open.

The Man in the Black Coat

This is a personal ghost story.

During my investigations, I've come upon many things that defy explanation. The world seems so real, so solid and complete, that I often doubt my own experiences. In the harsh light of day, many things seem distant and dreamlike. Science tells us that the world is built on a firm structure of rules. Night follows day. Water is wet. Dead is dead. The sense of order and completeness is comforting, especially when things are chaotic or out of control. We crave order. If the universe is orderly, it can be mapped, charted, and quantified. It can be controlled, and that means we as humans can have some kind of control over it. We have the illusion of safety, and we can sleep at night. This is how we live our day-to-day lives.

But. Occasionally we turn a corner and walk out of the rational world. Something happens that defies explanation or categorization, and the image we sought to build up of an orderly and rational universe comes tumbling down like a house of cards. The illogical or supernatural invades, and the mind recoils in horror, unable to process what it has seen.

But we humans have a built-in survival mechanism. When we encounter something that defies explanation, we shut it away and forget about it. We bathe it in the rational light of day and laugh about it. We claim it was just a dream—a hallucination—a product of an overactive imagination. All of us have encountered something we can't explain. You probably have, at one time or another.

Do you remember?

The problem with looking for ghosts is that, sooner or later, you will find them. This is fine when the conditions are set up beforehand. You prepare yourself to see strange and unusual things, and you rationalize what you see. You impose order on your perceptions, and avoid giving too much thought to what it means.

But like I said, if you go looking for ghosts, you find them. Or they find you.

During the summer of my final year at Ball State University, I spent a great deal of time taking late night walks around the campus, as well as the town surrounding it. The weather was warm, even at night, and the solitude gave me time to think. I would make long, rambling circles around the area, venturing out into the nearby neighborhoods and parks. One part of my circuit followed the railroad tracks for some small distance. The tracks ran through an area south of the campus for several miles before crossing the river and heading east into unknown territory. I would follow them for about a mile, walking on the ties, until I came to the bridge over the river. Then I would turn away and begin following the road again. The other side of the river was shrouded by trees, and I didn't know if it was private property or not.

On one particular night, I decided to dare the bridge. There were wooden guardrails and narrow platforms on each side of the tracks, so I wasn't afraid of encountering a train halfway across. I hurried along the distance all the same, not wanting to attract the attention of anyone on the nearby road. Once I got across, I saw that the way ahead was a corridor of tracks bound on both sides by trees and foliage. It ran straight east, into the distance, for what might have been miles; a hidden road amidst an ocean of darkness.

It was then that I saw the figure walking toward me along the tracks. It was some distance away still, and looked like nothing more than the silhouette of a person, headed in my direction. From the outline, I guessed it was a tall man in a long coat or duster. On his head I could see the outline of a wide-brimmed hat. He was moving toward the bridge. I suddenly didn't want him to see me or pass me on the tracks.

Looking back, I can almost tell myself this was a natural reaction. I was on the railroad tracks in the middle of the night. Whoever was headed toward me might be a drifter, or a drunkard, or any other number of dangerous and unfriendly people. But this is not true. I wasn't thinking of any of that at the time. There was just something about the man that made me want to not be seen by him.

The railroad tracks were on a raised embankment bordered on both sides by thick bushes and vines. I pushed my way through the bushes on my right and scrambled down the embankment until I was on flat ground again. I looked around for somewhere to hide, and finally realized where I was.

The trees on that side of the river were thick, and I had never before gotten a look at what lay beyond. I had driven by from the other side before, but my picture of the town was still fuzzy, and I had never put the two pieces of knowledge together.

I was in a cemetery.

I was surprised, but not frightened. Despite modern superstitions, most cemeteries are quiet and peaceful at night. There ARE a few exceptions, including one alarming little graveyard off the Eaton-Wheeling Pike, but for the most part, cemeteries are safe. This cemetery in particular was a large, sprawling area of land bisected by the railroad embankment, and it was unfamiliar to me. I hunted around until I found a nearby tree, and crouched behind it to wait.

A minute passed. Then two. The moon was obscured by clouds, and my eyes began to ache from staring into the darkness. I was looking around the tree at the swath of track visible above the bushes, waiting for the man to pass so I could continue on my way. My ankles were beginning to ache from crouching. Time crawled along, and still the man did not appear.

I finally stood up and crept back toward the tracks. I could see no one from my place at the bottom of the embankment, so I climbed back up through the bushes and stood on the tracks, looking in both directions. There was no one to be seen. Fair enough, I thought. The man had been pretty far ahead on the tracks. He had probably turned off at the road somewhere.

I continued on my walk, and encountered no one else that night.

Two nights later, I went walking again. I took my usual route around campus, and I found myself again on the railroad tracks. I followed them east until they crossed the river, then stopped. I looked out across the river at the dark corridor through the cemetery. There was a half moon that night, and it cast a dim, watery light on the tracks. I felt an odd foreboding about the land on the other side of the river. There was nothing visibly different about it, but it had some hidden sense of menace that night. It was as though there was a world lying behind the swath of darkness, projecting an aura of dread. I should have turned away and followed the road, or gone back the way I came.

I didn't.

I hurried across the bridge, onto the track that crossed the cemetery. I started walking, listening to my feet crunch on the gravel, then thump on the railroad ties. A breeze had kicked up that night, and it stirred the branches of the trees above me. I caught sight of movement ahead of me and looked up.

It was the man in the black coat.

He was closer this time, maybe fifty feet ahead. I looked at the silhouette approaching me and I was suddenly afraid. Something was very wrong. I felt cold despite the warmth of the night, and the only clear thought I had was that the man must not, must NOT see me. I jumped off from the embankment, just barely clearing the bushes, and landed in the wet grass of the cemetery. I got up and scrambled around behind my tree, crouching down as low as I could. I mustn't be seen, but I HAD to see him, to know he wasn't moving in my direction. If he had seen me, and followed me into the cemetery...

My breath was very loud in my ears. I had to stay still. I had to be silent and hope the man passed me by. Even if he had seen me, he might not know where I had gone. I just had to wait, and watch for him to pass by.

A minute passed. Then two.

And then he was there, on the tracks, passing by my hiding place. He walked in slow, measured steps, his coat fluttering around him. There was something wrong about it. It was his walk, or him, or something else I couldn't place. I couldn't make out his features, or anything about him. He was still a silhouette, nothing more than a shadow with the shape of a man.

And then I realized what was wrong about him.

I was only thirty feet back from the embankment, and the night had gone still. I should have heard his footsteps crunching on gravel or thumping on the railroad ties. I heard nothing at all.

The man stopped walking. He turned, slowly, until his silhouette was facing my hiding place. My breath caught in my throat, and I could somehow FEEL that shadow looking at me. There was a long, terrible pause as we regarded at each other. I saw nothing of him. No features. Nothing. Just a shadow of a man…or something *like* a man, looking at me in the dark.

The moment passed, and the man turned away and began walking. I started breathing again. I felt dizzy and disoriented, as though the whole scene was not quite real. I came out of my hiding place and ran to the tracks. I was terrified that I would see the man looking back at me, or turning to pursue me, but I had to know. I had to see.

I looked out over the bridge in the direction he had gone. It was empty.

There was no way the man could have crossed the bridge in that space of time. There was nowhere he could have gone.

I ran back across the bridge, then. I ran in the direction of civilization and I did not look back to see if anything was watching me. I wanted light and safety. I wanted to be somewhere things made sense.

I did not sleep well that night.

I have no idea what I saw. I don't know what it meant. But I have to trust my senses, and I know I saw—and felt—something terrifying that night. And it saw me.

I have not returned to that place. I have not crossed the bridge again, and I tend to avoid walking on the railroad tracks these days. I am an investigator by nature, but there are some places where I dare not go. We have instincts, buried deep, that keep us from wandering too far from our tiny circle of light and life. These instincts keep us safe… usually. I wonder, sometimes, about the people who disappear, and are not seen again. There are more than people think. No, I have not returned to that cemetery.

Whatever walks there, walks alone.

Mounds State Park

Few places in the state of Indiana have as long—or as uncertain—a history as Mounds State Park, and the earthworks it surrounds. The mounds were first recognized in the early 1800s, during land surveys. Frederick Bronnenburg purchased the land in 1821, and continued to look after it until his death in 1853. In 1879, the land was briefly owned by the Union Traction Company, which developed it into an amusement park. An unknown amount of damage to the mounds was done during this—luckily—short time, amusement parks being what they are.

Eventually, the mounds, including the Great Mound—which is the largest in the park—were excavated and examined by Indiana University. Within were found burials, log tombs, crematory basins, pits for refuse, and pottery. The carbon dating for the site puts it right around the beginning of the Christian Era, and the pottery is believed to be of Hopewell origin. The Hopewell were a tribe of people predating the more well-known Native American tribes who lived in the Indiana Area. The mounds were long suspected to be burial pits, but further research suggests that they may actually have been observatories to track the stars.

This would have been several decades prior to the birth of Christ, if the dating is correct. The mounds have alignments which lead archeologists to believe they were tied in with the longest and shortest days of the year. This demonstrates a remarkable degree of advancement for the civilization that built them, and has caused some controversy between professionals.

The people responsible for these creations are known as the Adena and Hopewell. Their culture is a mystery, as there are no written records, and very little evidence remains of who they were and how they lived. Their burial mounds/observatories exhibit a staggering degree of sophistication for the age, however. In fact, it is now believed by some that the whole complex was designed as a massive calendar-computer, and that it charts the position of the sun day-to-day.

Mounds Park has always been a high-activity area, and reports have ranged up and down the spectrum of strangeness. Some of the spirits seem clearly to be from people who have lived in the area in the last two centuries. Phantasms of a woman have been described around the still-standing house that belonged to the Bronnenburgs, as well as a "servant" spirit in overalls, and other less identifiable figures. The attic in particular is the subject of many reports, and has been reported as "draining" by sensitive people who have spent time inside.

Around the mounds themselves, all sorts of strange happenings have been reported. Accounts of lost time and strange, dancing lights abound, especially at night. The mounds seem to have a sort of low-level magnetism, and many people have had difficulty standing up after sitting for some time on or around them. Strangest of all, little blue-gowned dwarves or gnomes have been reported by more than one source, both on the mounds and over along the White River. This is interesting, because the description seems to correspond to Delaware Indian legend.

In the legend, they were called the Puk-wud-ies, and were considered to be a tribe of little people who inhabited the forest. They, along with other "nature spirits," are common in and around the mounds—both during the day and at night. The most frequent activity has been recorded around dusk.

Whatever the reason, and whatever purpose they may have had, the mounds give off a sense of great power and mystery. During my investigation, I noticed that there seemed to be a low-level humming, more felt than heard, which appeared to increase with the coming of dusk. There was a great sense of age about the place, and many shapes moved, seen out of the corners of my eyes while I sat beneath one of the trees near the Great Mound. Unlike many of the investigations I have been a part of, I felt no fear, even when it began to grow dark.

I did not encounter any of the Puk-wud-ies, but I would not have been surprised at the time if I had. The park feels quite removed from the "normal" world without, and had a blue-clad dwarf chanced to appear over the rise, I don't think I would have batted an eye.

If the mounds are, indeed, some kind of solar calculator, questions come up about how the Hopewell Indians could have engineered such technology. Perhaps they were assisted by the spirits, in which case the Puk-wud-ies may be guarding this strange remnant of a long-ago world. No records exist, so we may never know.

If you are traveling through the Anderson area, and have an interest in either history or spirituality, I would urge you to visit Mounds Park. It is open to the public for a number of hours, and during warmer months is an enchanting place to walk or sit in. Keep your eyes open while you are there, and you may chance to see one of the "little people." If you do, don't disturb them. They've been there longer than we have, after all.

Central State Hospital

There are certain places that are bursting with supernatural activity. Often nobody knows why, or the occurrences have been happening for as long as anyone can remember. It might be a bar, a house, or an abandoned building. It might be in the middle of the city, or deep in the lonely woods. The fact remains: Some places are VERY haunted.

Indianapolis is rife with ghosts and ghost stories. One of the most famous of these is the tale of Central State Hospital, and the events that happened—and are still happening—there. The Indiana Hospital for the Insane was opened in 1848, and remained open until the 1970s, when some of the buildings were found to be structurally unsound, and were torn down. In 1994, the hospital itself was closed to make way for more modern methods of treatment.

According to legend, some patients were treated in terrible and inhumane ways by the staff. Patients who were considered to be dangerous or "criminally insane" were kept in restraints on an almost constant basis, and housed in the dungeon-like basement of the hospital. Reports from the time indicate that the basements were dark, excessively damp, and foul-smelling.

There are also rumors that a patient committed suicide on the grounds. Sometime in the 1950s, workers who were renovating the underground tunnels are reputed to have found manacles and chains still hanging in some of the areas. Overall, the institution has a reputation for having a dark and unpleasant past.

Not surprisingly, there are numerous reports and stories concerning the unquiet dead in this defunct complex. The buildings itself stands in an area of Indianapolis that is far from the glaring lights of the inner city. The area is bathed in shadow, and the omnipresent sounds of city life are far, far in the distance. Possibly in another country. Or another world. It is said the voices of the inmates are heard whispering and crying out at dusk, begging for release or peace.

Reports of these distant and unearthly voices have come down from numerous people, including security guards and former employees of the institution. One area of the complex in particular has been cited as having a lot of this activity. A patient was at one time stoned to death by another patient in the area, and cries that very well might have come from the deceased are often heard in the vicinity.

The same guards and employees who have reported the voices have also played witness to spectral forms rushing out the doors and through the gates, as though escaping. Workers in the boiler rooms of the complex have also seen what they thought were moving shadows, darting around the columns in the darkened space.

The most alarming report, however, comes from one worker who was taking a short nap one night in the basement. According to the man, he was awakened by the sensation of hands around his throat, choking him. He wrestled free of the unseen hands and switched on the light, but no one was there. He might have put the experience down to a frightening dream, or his own overactive imagination, but when he pulled down the neck of his shirt, he found angry red marks where the hands had been.

There are numerous other reports of sounds—especially treading footsteps—and unexplained events, including machines turning on by themselves, flashlights spontaneously going out, and knocking sounds coming from above and below.

I was unable to do a full investigation, but inspection of the grounds and reports from previous workers and other investigators lends a great deal of validity to this haunted locale. If you are in the Indianapolis area, and have an interest in visiting the supernatural and strange, I highly recommend paying Central State Hospital a visit.

Malloy's Pub

Malloy's Pub is a staple of the Fort Wayne area. The building it is housed in is over one hundred years old, and may have been a telephone company, a speakeasy, and a coal storage building in its time. The building next door burnt down some years ago. The incidents that have taken place have been reported by at least three employees and two patrons, and the owner himself has taken a personal interest in the affair. The disturbances haven't been frightening or violent, and there's no indication that any spirits are angry—unlike Central State—but there has been a high level of activity in recent years. In a series of three months, eleven "major events" were recorded. These include sightings, moving objects, and obvious sounds reported by workers and patrons. Numerous smaller events take place every day as well. The owner himself tells a story of an orb (a glowing ball of light) responding to the presence of people while on camera, and people have reported odd occurrences such as pool balls stopping on their own during a game. There seems to be no end to the reports of experiences in the area of the pub.

Subsequent investigations have produced even further evidence of activity, especially of strange and unexplained occurrences. Batteries will die even at full power, cellular phones will light up on their own—with no incoming calls. Many people have felt figures brushing up against them on various occasions, or seen something like a heat shimmer moving on its own.

My final judgment on Malloy's Pub is pending further investigation, but like Central State, all reports point to a heavy amount of supernatural activity in and around the area. It's enough to make one wonder what the spot the pub is on has that draws in so much spiritual turbulence. However, if you happen to be in Vigo County, or the Fort Wayne area sometime soon, the pub is definitely worth a visit.

Comparing Central State and Malloy's Pub

Both Central State and Malloy's, are famous for their high levels of activity, and their interactions with visitors and employees alike. In the case of Central State, the reason for this may be partially explained, but why Malloy's? What makes one place spiritually active over another?

This, like the nature of the spirits and the question of their consciousness, is another unknown factor in the search for understanding ghosts and hauntings.

On Poltergeists

Special Note: Both authors have had eerie experiences with poltergeists, even at the same location in this case!

There has been a lot of debate lately about whether poltergeists should be counted as ghosts along with traditional hauntings. Can there, after all, be a ghost if no spirit, apparition, or shade ever appears? There are hauntings without a visible ghost, after all. However, poltergeist activity is different in a number of ways. Current opinion is that poltergeists are an entirely different phenomenon, and possibly not caused by entities of any kind.

A poltergeist (literally "Noisy Ghost") is a brief, violent episode that usually centers around a house, a family, or a specific person. Unlike hauntings, which can last for centuries, poltergeist activity tends to occur for only a few months, or even a few weeks. The episodes are characterized by a variety of activity, most often objects moving by themselves, lights turning on or off, rappings or bangings that have no source, and other strange sounds around the area. People can sometimes be attacked in their sleep or scratched, and in some cases unexplained wounds or bruises appear on members of the household.

Most researchers agree that poltergeist activity is rarely related to any identifiable ghosts or spirits. The activity doesn't involve any specific presence or entity, and no figures are seen during the time. Poltergeists are sometimes compared to—or mistaken for—demon possession, due to the violent events that characterize both.

Most poltergeist activity seems to happen to or around one person in the household, and sometimes even goes away when that person is out of the house. The afflicted person is most often female and adolescent, and often suffers from emotional trouble or instability. This has led some people to suggest a link between adolescence and poltergeist activity. The girl, they say, could be causing the disturbances unconsciously, as her mind and body change with the onset of puberty. While there is no way to prove if this is true, studies of PK (PsychoKinetic—meaning the moving of objects or causing of things to happen with the mind alone) in adolescents show a surprising amount of ability during that time. The link between puberty and poltergeist activity would also explain the short duration of the disturbances.

Probably the most famous use of the word "Poltergeist" is in the 1982 Tobe Hooper/Steven Spielberg movie of the same name. While much of what occurs is unrelated to normal poltergeist activity, and is blown far out of proportion, the early portion of the movie gives a decent portrayal of what a poltergeist disturbance might be like. Objects move on their own, often while no one is looking at them, sliding around or stacking themselves on tables. A room shakes in the middle of the night, and banging sounds are heard all around the house. Voices speak to the youngest child in the middle of the night, voices which only she can hear. All of these things are classic indicators of poltergeist activity, and are well-portrayed before the movie veers off into more fantastic and uncommon occurrences.

The poltergeist phenomenon, while easily as well-documented as traditional hauntings, remains somewhat in the background of the paranormal world. It may be that sharp, shocking incidents which give no suggestion of someone's grandmother sending messages back from the afterlife are less interesting to many people than their calmer counterpoints (although the case of Central State Hospital is far from calm).

Indianapolis, always a haven for the strange and supernatural, was host to a particularly alarming poltergeist experience in March of 1962. A house on Delaware Street, occupied by a small and turbulent family, was the central area. The events began suddenly and violently, with items falling off of shelves, flying across the room, and leaping from tabletops. Most surprising was how quickly the events began, and how often they occurred. Several of these happened in one night, and the family living there was frightened enough to leave the house for the evening.

As is characteristic of poltergeist activity, they returned to find that nothing had been disturbed in their absence. Once they were back, however, objects started hurling themselves about the house again. In desperation, the family called the police, who suggested the damage could have been done by some kind of stereo noise, or a pellet gun. What was more alarming, by that time, were the puncture wounds that had begun appearing on the hands and arms of two of the family members. They resembled something that might have been made by a bat, or some other small creature, but none had been seen by anyone in the house, or by any of the police officers.

The next day, an officer arrived for a tour of the damages, including a smashed mirror—shattered by an ashtray that had flown across the room—and a set of what used to be six matched glasses, from which three had broken of their own accord, then disappeared. Just as he was leaving, however, one of the missing glasses hit him in the back hard enough to leave a bruise, and shattered.

These events went on for several days, by which time they had both peaked and subsided with surprising speed. The house ransacked by the end, strewn with broken glass, smashed mirrors, and gouges in the walls where things had been thrown around.

Once the disturbance quieted, the clean-up effort began, and the stricken family tried to put their lives back together. Through their later years, they were plagued by efforts to deny and explain away their experiences, despite the evidence of strange goings-on. Was the incident the result of the family's daughter? Was there some other unexplained factor at work? Did the turbulent family somehow tap into some other kind of energy and expend their violence in a way they never normally could? We have no answers, and if there were any ghosts involved in the Delaware Street incident, they certainly aren't talking.

In another case, a family on the north side of Indianapolis was troubled for months by an on-and-off disturbance in their house. The incidents started in February, with unexplained bangings and scratchings on the wall. The family had their house investigated by exterminators and other professionals, but no reason could be found for the sounds. These continued for weeks, growing steadily worse, until the family had trouble sleeping at night.

The sounds were particularly loud in the daughter's room, and when they moved her bed to a spare room, the knockings seemed to follow her there. Not long after the sounds reached their peak, the china plates in one particular cabinet jumped off their shelf and smashed onto the floor. The girl's mother was in the kitchen at the time and reported the cabinet as having opened by itself.

Later that night, the family found a heavy chair overturned on the living room rug. This family, however, did not call the police over the affair, and only told their story after the events had taken place. For several nights after the chair was overturned, the daughter claimed her bed was shaking or bumping around at night, usually waking her when she was already asleep.

On one particular occasion, the girl's mother came into the room during the middle of the incident, and saw the bed actually shaking around. The girl ended up sharing a bed with her mother, and the shaking incidents stopped.

For a while, things continued in this same vein. Things would be thrown around or overturned day to day, but never too many, or too violently. The knockings on the wall continued, but grew no worse.

Then, in April, the disturbances intensified. Members of the family would wake up to find scratches on their arms or necks. Stains and pools of water would sometimes appear inexplicably on the carpet, or on the linoleum in the kitchen. One day, a cup of coffee flew off the counter and hit the girl's father, scalding him.

The family, desperate for help, called in paranormal investigators. The investigators arrived, and spent several days in the house witnessing and recording the incidents. Apart from the obvious, they observed that certain rooms, especially the daughter's bedroom, would experience sudden drops in pressure just before an event. Though they spent several nights sleeping in the house, they were neither attacked, nor scratched. One of the three individuals did say that a book jumped off a shelf and nearly struck him in the head as he was walking by, but none of the others were attacked.

Over the next month the disturbances wound down, and by the end of May, things were back to normal. The family went on with their lives, and since then have had no further incidents. Like the previous case, it remains a mystery. Poltergeist disturbances appear seemingly out of nowhere, and then dry up and disappear so fast, investigators often rush to the scene to get what readings they can. Disturbances lasting as little as a day have been recorded, and a very scant few have lasted years. So far as we know, there are no verified instances of a poltergeist disturbance going on indefinitely—unlike hauntings, that have quite a few multi-generation reports, and even a few whose existence goes back as far as old folklore. There's a feeling among people who study poltergeists, much like tornado chasers, that their time to collect data is limited, and their subject can appear anywhere, at any time.

Poltergeist incidents, as mentioned before, can be particularly disturbing to those who are familiar with, or looking for, incidents of demon possession. Many of the things that happen in poltergeist disturbances mirror some of the aspects of demon possession. As a result of the most famous (or infamous) demon possession movie ever made—*The Exorcist*—many people have got a skewed idea of what most demonic encounters are like.

Quite a few of the victims of demon possession never lose control of their minds, nor do they always project the voice of the demon through themselves. This does happen sometimes, but more frequently the subject is attacked, from without and within, by the presence. This includes wounds on the body, bruises, and being thrown around by unseen forces. Sometimes the afflicted person is shaken violently, or feels as though things around them are shaking. This even appears in the movie *The Exorcist*, when young Reagan's bed shakes and thumps around violently. Some instances of demonic possession have involved objects moving—or breaking—on their own, as well.

No one is certain whether there is a connection between the sinister world of demonic possession, and the alarming—but certainly less dread-inducing—world of the poltergeist. The two are closely related, and both center on an individual—quite often a troubled young girl—who find themselves the focus of whatever supernatural activity is taking place. It can be said that poltergeists are (usually) less violent toward individuals, but if both kinds of disturbances are a spectrum, with poltergeists at one end, and demons at the other, this would go a long way toward explaining the difference.

For whatever reason, poltergeists remain a topic of secondary interest to most ghost hunters and investigators. Whether this is due to its ephemeral nature, the lack of a notable ghost or spirit presence, or some kind of deeply-buried survival instinct is beyond by knowledge. Whatever the reason may be, poltergeists remain in the background of supernatural experience, a shadow of the unknown.

The Rivoli Theater

The Rivoli was the first Universal Studios theater built in Indianapolis, back in the year 1927. It was a snazzy place for its day and age, made of the finest materials available, and patterned in the popular Spanish mission style. At the time it was built, eastern Indianapolis was still considered fairly rural, and some people wondered at the seating accommodations for 1,500 people. For a "neighborhood" theater, that was a surprising capacity. In terms of pure acoustic space, the Rivoli was also second to none. Many theater productions were put on there, due to the stage, which was the largest in Indianapolis.

Unfortunately for history, the Rivoli was sold in 1937, when Universal could no longer maintain its upkeep. It passed from owner to owner, and was sometimes neglected, but never stayed buried for too long. Motion pictures and live performances—including music concerts—continued there until the early nineties.

In 1992, the Rivoli finally closed for good. It sits empty now, but is expected to eventually be designated a historical location. Plans are still in the works to go in and revamp the aging theater, and perhaps have concerts and plays and movies there again, someday.

The theater itself still gives off an air of bygone, glamorous, and rose-colored days. The suit of armor that stands in the lobby can be seen from out on the street, and the concessions counter and—of course—the popcorn machine are still inside. The building looks,

to all impressions, to be sleeping. Perhaps it is. If buildings have personalities—and they do—the Rivoli seems
to be deep in slumber, listening to the echoes of long-
ago movies that can still be heard in the quiet, empty
auditoriums.

We forget that theaters were once high-toned affairs,
that people dressed up in their best clothes to go see the
old movies. A movie premiere was once a social carnival,
and everyone in the neighborhood would show up to
discuss it in the lobby and reconnect with old friends.

Maybe it is this wealth of memory and almost talis-
manic social significance that gives theaters of all kinds
their power, as well as their ghosts. For whatever reasons,
theaters are common places for hauntings, and when the
news comes out, people are rarely surprised. After all,
there's something about a big, old theater that feels a bit
like a big Victorian mansion. If the one can have ghosts,
we think, surely the other is at least more likely to play
host to the supernatural. It's an illogical comparison, but
it seems this time, we're right. Whether by luck, by some
kind of unknown paranormal stereotype, or because we
expect it, theaters are almost always havens of some kind
of ghost. The Rivoli is no exception.

Several different owners have told stories about the
supernatural goings-on at the Rivoli. One of the most
common incidents seemed to happen early in the day,
when the owners arrived to open the place up. They
would look into the auditorium and see people sitting
in the seats as though waiting for a show. The surprised
owner would go into the auditorium to confront these
people, and before his eyes they would disappear. Patrons to the theater would sometimes claim to see a
figure running down the aisle, who would eventually
disappear into the wall. No one was sure who this phan-

tom man was, but there were numerous reports of him down through the years.

Charles Chulchian purchased the Rivoli in 1976, which was when many of the strange events began happening. He had heard stories from previous owners and moviegoers about the Rivoli being haunted, but had dismissed them as imagination. As time went on, however, he began to suspect there was more to the "haunted" theater than he had previously thought.

There were instances where patrons claimed to see a man in a tuxedo and a woman in a dress sitting in the theater, apparently waiting for the show to start. This was odd, because the patrons reporting this incident were the first to arrive, and no other tickets had been sold. When someone went to investigate the mysterious man and woman, they were nowhere to be found.

For some reason, the women's restroom played host to a number of strange occurrences. Many people claimed to be uncomfortable or ill at ease in the restroom, as though they were being watched. Others saw the faucets turn themselves on and off, heard sounds from empty stalls, or saw movement that turned out to be nothing. One report in particular told of a woman who had appeared in the mirror, but was not in the bathroom at the time.

The staff at the movie theater were also ill at ease. They saw many odd things, including items moving on their own or appearing in different places without having been moved. Sometimes they were "pushed" or touched by someone who was not there. Most of the staff refused to clean the auditorium alone, because they felt some kind of force or presence was in the room with them. Chulchian had trouble keeping workers on a long-term basis, since many of them became frightened or intimidated by whatever spirit or spirits lived in the aging theater. Even Chulchian himself was present once when he and an employee watched a water faucet turn on and off by itself. There was no denying the strange and inexplicable events.

During his time as the owner of the Rivoli, Chulchian worked to repair the theater and mend many of the places that time and neglect had decayed. He would sometimes work late into the night, fixing and maintaining the many mechanical and technical aspects of the theater. On one particular occasion, Chulchian was working late fixing a boiler when the room grew suddenly cold. A moment later, he felt arms wrapping around him from behind. He turned around, startled, but there was no one else in the room. At that time of night, alone in the dark, it's no surprise that Chulchian was frightened enough to run. He later said it was the only time the ghostly occurrences got the best of him.

The interruptions and strange happenings continued, often while Chulchian was working alone on the theater. He would hear strange sounds, experience cold snaps, and find that objects were moving by themselves, or were in places he had not left them.

Finally, he decided one day to bring in an infra-red camera and film the auditorium. He set the camera up in the projection booth and aimed it out at the empty auditorium, which was fully darkened. Both Chulchian and a friend who had accompanied him witnessed a light appearing in the theater, forming into the shape of a man, and then collapsing several minutes later.

Nor was this the only report of a person-shaped figure of light. Later that very week, a friend of Chulchian's saw a ghostly man and woman on the projection booth stairs. In fact, the projection room seemed to become a focus for strange visitations, along with the auditorium. Chulchian was working late up in the projection booth and caught sight of someone in his peripheral vision, who he took at first to be an employee. He asked a question, and when he got no answer, he looked up to find that he was alone. He suspected later that he had seen the lady ghost of the theater, a spectral woman many people have reported encountering.

The Rivoli theater has been closed for several years, but Mr. Chulchian is still the owner, and he still looks after his building. As of this writing, he still encounters the ghostly lady, and many of the other strange happenings, on a regular basis. In fact, the activity seems to have increased with the theater being unoccupied. Items disappear and reappear on a regular basis, lights turn on and off, and stranger happenings have been reported as well.

The known history of the building, as well as the area it was built on, is peppered with accounts of unexplained occurrences and spectral encounters. Perhaps there is something about the very ground the theater is on that attracts and augments supernatural activity. Possibly, like many people believe, there are unseen lines—ley lines—that run all across the earth, and where these lines intersect is where strange and unexplained things happen. If that is true, perhaps the Rivoli Theater was built on just such an intersection. We may never know.

Whatever the reason, the Rivoli is a VERY haunted Indianapolis locale, and worth a look, if you are in the neighborhood.

Outro

There are places where we dare not go. I mean this both literally and figuratively. We find these no-where places both in our own minds and in the wide world. Something, some instinct from the deepest part of our consciousness tells us to stay away, keep back, don't investigate further. Whatever waits for us in those nowhere places is something to be feared, our instincts tell us. So we stay away, keep back, or turn our attention to more comfortable things. And the world stays safe for a little while.

But we can't avoid the darkness forever, because it is inside as well as outside. There are places in your mind where you do not go, either consciously or instinctually. You might recognize some of these places, if you are of an introspective bent. Others are empty doorways, and the corridors they open onto are unknown. These are the places from which nightmares come. They are inside every one of us.

And outside, too, as we have tried to convey in this book. Haunted houses and unhallowed grounds can be found by those who go looking, or those unlucky enough to stumble on them, and there too is the twilight place. The rational, sunlit world we inhabit day to day meets the world of the irrational, the insane, and the monstrous, and sometimes there is space between the two. This is where we cross over into things we cannot explain: The haunting, the possession, the monstrous thing glimpsed for a moment through a window. The shadow on the wall. These are emissaries from the outer darkness, scions of a world where the laws that keep us sane from day to day dissolve and blow away on the howling wind.

In this twilight world, everything looks just as it does in the bright, rational light of day...except not quite right. Something is different, something is wrong. Some of the wrongness from that howling dark has leaked in through cracks in the doorway, and is here, now, with us. When it is gone we will forget it, discount it, even laugh at it. In the light of day it will seem ephemeral and foolish and unreal. But right here, right now, there is something *other* in the room with us. We are looking into the abyss...and it is looking back.

Sooner or later this happens to almost everyone, and when it does, almost everyone forgets it as soon as they can. Those people who go looking for it are considered aberrations, exceptions to the rule of con-trollable fear. Lots of people like scary movies. Plenty of people like roller coasters. Not so many people like hunting for ghosts. Even of those who DO go looking for the paranormal, most will shrink back upon actually encountering something strange. Because it's real, and it's from somewhere else, and that old human instinct is in the back of the mind is screaming that you have to RUN, you have to GET AWAY. People who venture too far or too often into those places get twitchy.

What all this means is unknown, but what it suggests is that we as a species are not ready yet to venture into the larger world outside our little circle of light. Again, I mean that both in a mental and physical sense. Men-tally, we aren't ready for the shock of those unmapped places, or of encountering things that tear our ordered concepts to pieces. Physically...there may be things out in the darkness, and if you don't think there are some dark and terrible entities hiding in the deep places of the world, I advise you to do some research. You may be unpleasantly surprised.

The stories and accounts in this book are meant to be entertaining, and if you read and enjoyed them, we have done our job. However, for those few of you who care about the great unknown, we hope they will also serve as a reminder: The paranormal is under and behind all the things we take for granted, and if you go looking for it, you will find it. And that's when things get interesting...

From Tom Baker and Jonathan Titchenal, Goodnight.

Top Ten Places to Find Ghosts

—Fiona Broome, http://hollowhill.com/

No matter where you are, certain locations are usually haunted. These sites don't always have ghosts, but they're the best places to start when you're looking for unreported visitors from beyond the grave.

Theatres

Ghosts frequent places where people have performed on stage. These include movie theatres that were once performance halls.

There are three kinds of ghosts at these locations:

First, at least one actor who is still seen on or near the stage.

Second, a stagehand lingers backstage, usually around the lighting or the curtain controls.

Finally, someone appears towards the back of the hall, especially during rehearsals. He or she almost always smokes a cigarette that people can smell, or they'll see the smoke or the burning ember.

Battlegrounds

Almost every battleground has some residual energy from the violent and tragic deaths that occurred there. Some battlegrounds are actually haunted by the spirits of the men and women who died there, too. Between Texas' battles for independence, Indian attacks, and Civil War conflicts, you'll find many locations with ghost stories… and real ghosts.

Cemeteries

It's a cliché but a true one: Ghosts haunt cemeteries. Modern graves—burials that occurred less than fifty years ago—are rarely haunted for very long.

For the most powerful hauntings, look for graves that are at least a hundred years old. Only a few are haunted, but you'll find elevated EMF levels at many of graves, especially if they're unmarked.

Colleges

Almost every college or university reports at least one ghost. Most also report poltergeist phenomena. The performing arts center is often the most haunted location on campus. In Austin, the University of Texas campus is probably the most haunted college.

Summer Camps

Most camps—especially Scout camps—have a ghost or two. Usually, these are benevolent ghosts of former camp counselors or the camp manager. An aroma of perfume or pipe smoke is usually reported, related to someone who worked there.

Very Old, Large Homes and Buildings

Like most ancient castles, many very old, large buildings have ghosts. In an older home, a woman who lived there lingers to be sure that the house and its occupants remain safe. She usually wears a green dress.

Another ghost is mad and lurks in the attic, basement, or an outbuilding. A variation on this is a ghost in the nearby woods or a field next to an old homestead. These hauntings are almost predictable.

Old Hotels

Many hotels are haunted by the same people who visited them in life. They're usually happy ghosts who return to relax and enjoy themselves.

Classic haunted spots in hotels include the top floor, the elevator, and the lobby. This is true of the Driskill Hotel, Austin's most haunted and elegant hotel, and a favorite destination for visiting ghost hunters.

Around Austin, this category of haunting extends to former brothels. In the late nineteenth century, dozens of feisty, independent-minded madams owned "boarding houses" around downtown Austin. Today, these sites are often clubs, bars, and restaurants in the entertainment and warehouse districts of Austin. And, most of them have great ghost stories to share.

Hospitals, Retirement Homes, Morgues and Funeral Parlors

As you'd expect, some people aren't willing to leave the last place where they were seen and called by name. However, if these sites are still in use, they're usually off-limits to ghost hunters.

Instead, look for former locations of these kinds of buildings. They're usually haunted by perplexed and sometimes angry ghosts.

Around Austin, there are probably hundreds of unreported ghosts. If you follow these suggestions, you'll find even more ghosts than are included in these pages.

* The following section is provided by the Chester County Paranormal Research Society in Pennsylvania and appears in training materials for new investigators.

Please visit www.ChesterCountyprs.com for more information.

Glossary

Air Probe Thermometer

A thermometer with an external probe that is capable of taking instant measurements of the air temperature.

Anomalous field

A field that can not be explained or ruled out by various possibilities, that can be a representation of spirit or paranormal energy present.

Apparition

A transparent form of a human or animal, a spirit.

Artificial field

A field that is caused by electrical outlets, appliances, etc.

Aural Enhancer

A listening device that enhances or amplifies audio signals. i.e., Orbitor Bionic Ear.

Automatic writing

The act of a spirit guiding a human agent in writing a message that is brought through by the spirit.

Base readings

The readings taken at the start of an investigation and are used as a means of comparing other readings taken later during the course of the investigation.

Demonic Haunting

A haunting that is caused by an inhuman or subhuman energy or spirit.

Dowsing Rods

A pair of L-shaped rods or a single Y-shaped rod, used to detect the presence of what the person using them is trying to find.

Electro-static generator

A device that electrically charges the air often used in paranormal investigations/research as a means to contribute to the materialization of paranormal or spiritual energy.

ELF

Extremely Low Frequency.

ELF Meter/EMF Meter

A device that measures electric and magnetic fields.

EMF

Electro Magnetic Field.

EVP

Electronic Voice Phenomena.

False positive

Something that is being interpreted as paranormal within a picture or video and is, in fact, a natural occurrence or defect of the equipment used.

Gamera

A 35mm film camera connected with a motion detector that is housed in a weather proof container and takes a picture when movement is detected. Made by Silver Creek Industries.

Geiger Counter

A device that measures gamma and x-ray radiation.

Infra Red

An invisible band of radiation at the lower end of the visible light spectrum. With wavelengths from 750 nm to 1 mm, infrared starts at the end of the microwave spectrum and ends at the beginning of visible light. Infrared transmission typically requires an unobstructed line of sight between transmitter and receiver. Widely used in most audio and video remote controls, infrared transmission is also used for wireless connections between computer devices and a variety of detectors.

Intelligent haunting

A haunting of a spirit or other entity that has the ability to interact with the living and do things that can make its presence known.

Milli-gauss

Unit of measurement, measures in 1000th of a gauss and is named for the famous German mathematician, Karl Gauss.

Orbs

Anomalous spherical shapes that appear on video and still photography.

Pendulum

A pointed item that is hung on the end of a string or chain and is used as a means of contacting spirits. An individual will hold the item and let it hang from the finger tips. The individual will ask questions aloud and the pendulum answers by moving.

Poltergeist haunting

A haunting that has two sides, but same kinds of activity in common. Violent outbursts of activity with doors and windows slamming shut, items being thrown across a room and things being knocked off of surfaces. Poltergeist hauntings are usually focused around a specific individual who resides or works at the location of the activity reported, and, in some cases, when the person is not present at the location, activity does not occur. A poltergeist haunting may be the cause of a human agent or spirit/energy that may be present at the location.

Portal

An opening in the realm of the paranormal that is a gateway between one dimension and the next. A passageway for spirits to come and go through. See also Vortex.

Residual haunting

A haunting that is an imprint of an event or person that plays itself out like a loop until the energy that causes it has burned itself out.

Scrying

The act of eliciting information with the use of a pendulum from spirits.

Table Tipping

A form of spirit communication, the act of a table being used as a form of contact. Individuals will sit around a table and lightly place there fingertips on the edge of the table and elicit contact with a spirit. The Spirit will respond by "tipping" or moving the table.

Talking Boards

A board used as a means of communicating with a spirit. Also known as a Quija Board.

Vortex

A place or situation regarded as drawing into its center all that surrounds it.

White Noise

A random noise signal that has the same sound energy level at all frequencies.

Equipment Explanations

In this section, the Chester County Paranormal Research Society looks at the application and benefits of equipment used on investigations with greater detail. The equipment used for an investigation plays a vital role in the ability to collect objective evidence and helps to determine what is and is not paranormal activity. But a key point to be made here is: the investigator is the most important tool on any investigation. With that said, let us now take a look at the main pieces of equipment used during an investigation...

The Geiger Counter

The Geiger counter is device that measures radiation. A "Geiger counter" usually contains a metal tube with a thin metal wire along its middle. The space in between them is sealed off and filled with a suitable gas and with the wire at about +1000 volts relative to the tube.

An ion or electron penetrating the tube (or an electron knocked out of the wall by X-rays or gamma rays) tears electrons off atoms in the gas. Because of the high positive voltage of the central wire, those electrons are then attracted to it. They gain energy that collide with atoms and release more electrons, until the process snowballs into an "avalanche", producing an easily detectable pulse of current. With a suitable filling gas, the flow of electricity stops by itself, or else the electrical circuitry can help stop it.

The instrument was called a "counter" because every particle passing it produced an identical pulse, allowing particles to be counted, usually electronically. But it did not tell anything about their identity or energy, except that they must have sufficient energy to penetrate the walls of the counter.

The Geiger counter is used in paranormal research to measure the background radiation at a location. The working theory in this field is that paranormal activity can effect the background radiation. In some cases, it will increase the radiation levels and in other cases it will decrease the levels.

Digital and 35mm Film Cameras

The camera is an imperative piece of equipment that enabled us to gather objective evidence during a case. Some of the best evidence presented from cases of paranormal activity over the years has been because of photographs taken. If you own your own digital camera or 35mm film camera, you need to be fully aware of what the cameras abilities and limitations are. Digital cameras have been at the center of great debate in the field of paranormal research over the years.

The earlier incarnations of digital cameras were full of inherent problems and notorious for creating "false positive" pictures. A "false positive" picture is a picture that has anomalous elements within the picture that are the result of a camera defect or other natural occurrence. There are many pictures scattered about the internet that claim to be of true paranormal activity, but in fact they are "false positives." Orbs, defined as anomalous paranormal energy that can show up as balls of light or streaks in still photography or video, are the most controversial pictures of paranormal energy in the field. There are so many theories (good and bad) about the origin of orbs and what they are. Every picture in the CCPRS collection that has an orb—or orbs—are not presented in a way that state that they are absolutely paranormal of nature. I have yet to capture an orb photo that made me feel certain that in fact it is of a paranormal nature.

If you use your own camera, understand that your camera is vital. I encourage all members who own their own cameras to do research on the make and model of the camera and see what other consumers are saying about them. Does the manufacturer give any info regarding possible defects or design flaws with that particular model? Understanding your camera will help to rule out the possibility of interpreting a "false positive" for an authentic picture of paranormal activity.

Video Cameras

The video camera is also a fundamental tool in the investigation as another way for collecting objective evidence that can support the proof of paranormal activity. The video camera can be used in various ways during the investigation. It can be set on a tripod and left in a location where paranormal activity has been reported. It can also be used as a hand-held camera and the investigator will take it with them during their walk through investigation as a means of documenting to hopefully capture anomalous activity on tape. Infra-Red technology has become a feature on most consumer level video cameras and depending on the manufacturer can be called "night shot" or "night alive." What this technology does is allow us to use the camera in zero light. Most cameras with this feature will add a green tint or haze to the camera when it is being used in this mode. A video camera with this ability holds great appeal to the paranormal investigator.

EMF/ELF Meters

EMF=Electro Magnetic Frequency   ELF=Extremely Low Frequency

What is an EMF/ELF meter? Good question. The EMF/ELF meter is a meter that measures Electric and Magnetic fields in an AC or DC current field. It measures in a unit of measurement called "milli-gauss," named for the famous German mathematician, Karl Gauss. Most meters will measure in a range of 1-5 or 1-10 milli-gauss. The reason that EMF meters are used in paranormal research is because of the theory that a spirit or paranormal energy can add to the energy field when it is materializing or is present in a location. The theory says that, typically, an energy that measures between 3-7 milli-gauss may be of a paranormal origin. This doesn't mean that an artificial field can't also measure within this range. That is why we take base readings and make maps notating where artificial fields occur. The artificial fields are a direct result of electricity, i.e. wiring, appliances, light switches, electrical outlets, circuit breakers, high voltage power lines, sub-stations, etc.

The Earth emits a naturally occurring magnetic field all around us and has an effect on paranormal activity. Geo-magnetic storm activity can also have a great influence on paranormal activity. For more information on this kind of phenomena visit: www.noaa.sec.com.

There are many different types of EMF meters; and each one, although it measures with the same unit of measurement, may react differently. An EMF meter can range from anywhere to $12.00 to $1,000.00 or more depending on the quality and features that it has. Most meters are measuring the AC (alternating current, the type of fields created by man-made electricity) fields and some can measure DC (direct current-naturally occurring fields, batteries also fall into the category of DC) fields. The benefit of having a meter that can measure DC fields is that they will automatically filter out the artificial fields created by AC fields and can pick up more naturally occurring electro magnetic fields. Some of the higher-tech EMF meters are so sensitive that they can pick up the fields generated by living beings. The EMF meter was originally designed to measure the earth's magnetic fields and also to measure the fields created by electrical an artificial means.

There have been various studies over the years about the long term effects of individuals living in or near high fields. There has been much controversy as to whether or not long term exposure to high fields can lead to cancer. It has been proven though that no matter what, long term exposure to high fields can be harmful to your health. The ability to locate these high fields within a private residence or business is vital to the investigation. We may offer suggestions to the client as to possible solutions for dealing with high fields. The wiring in a home or business can greatly affect the possibility of high fields. If the wiring is old and/or not shielded correctly, it can emit high fields that may affect the ability to correctly notate any anomalous fields that may be present.

Audio Recording Equipment

Audio recording equipment is used for conducting EVP (Electronic Voice Phenomena) research and experiments. What is an EVP? An EVP is a phenomenon where paranormal voices or sounds can be captured with audio recording devices. The theory is that the activity will imprint directly onto the device or tape, but has not been proven to be an absolute fact. The use of an external microphone is essential when conducting EVP experiments with analog recording equipment. The internal microphone on an analog tape recorder can pick up the background noise of the working parts within the tape recorder and can taint the evidence as a whole. Most digital recorders are quiet enough to use the internal microphone, but as a general rule of thumb, we do not use them. An external microphone will be used always. Another theory about EVP research is that an authentic EVP will happen within the range 250-400hz. This is a lower frequency range and isn't easily heard by the human ear, and the human voice does not emit in this range. EVP is rarely heard at the moment it happens—it is usually revealed during the playback and analysis portion of the investigation.

Thermometers

The use of a thermometer in an investigation goes without saying. This is how we monitor the temperature changes during the course of an investigation. CCPRS is currently using Digital thermometers with remote sensors as a way to set up a perimeter and to notate any changes in a stationary location of an investigation. The Air-probe thermometer can take "real time" readings that are instantly accurate. This is the more appropriate thermometer for measuring air temperature and "cold spots" that may be caused by the presence of paranormal phenomena. The IR Non-contact thermometer is the most misused thermometer in the field of paranormal research. CCPRS does not own or use IR Non-contact thermometers for this reason. The IR (infra-red) Non-contact thermometer is meant for measuring surface temperatures from a remote location. It shoots an infrared beam out to an object and bounces to the unit and gives the temperature reading. I have seen, first hand, investigators using this thermometer as a way to measure air temperature. NO, this is not correct! Enough said. In an email conversation that I have had with Grant Wilson from TAPS, he has said that, "Any change in temperature that can't be measured with your hand is not worth notating..."